Born for the Road

Born for the Road

My Story So Far

NATHAN CARTER

with Emma Heatherington

PENGUIN
IRELAND

PENGUIN IRELAND

UK | USA | Canada | Ireland | Australia
India | New Zealand | South Africa

Penguin Ireland is part of the Penguin Random House group of companies
whose addresses can be found at global.penguinrandomhouse.com.

First published 2018
001

Set in 13.5/16 pt Garamond MT Std
Typeset by Jouve (UK), Milton Keynes
Printed and bound in Great Britain by Clays Ltd, Elcograf S.p.A.

A CIP catalogue record for this book is available from the British Library

ISBN: 978–1–844–88447–6

www.greenpenguin.co.uk

Penguin Random House is committed to a
sustainable future for our business, our readers
and our planet. This book is made from Forest
Stewardship Council® certified paper.

For my family
With love and thanks for being with me
every step of the way

Nathan says thanks to:

Mum, Dad, Jake, Kiara, Nan and Grumps for giving me so many wonderful memories in life so far.

John Farry, for his guidance, belief, vision and continued confidence in my career.

My band and crew for your friendship and support and for sharing your own stories of life on the road.

All the Irish and UK media, concert and gig promoters, venue owners and my fellow country artists, whose comments were so kind and supportive. It's a pleasure working with you all.

The staff at Corick House and Country Spa, County Tyrone for accommodating us on early writing sessions for *Born for the Road*.

Michael McLoughlin, Claire Pelly and all at Penguin Ireland for this wonderful opportunity to write my book.

Emma Heatherington for putting my life story into words with humour and emotion (even if it did make my Mum cry!).

And finally, a huge thanks to all of my fans who sent in stories and for being with me every step of the way. I hope you enjoy my story so far.

Lots of love,
Nathan

Contents

At the age of just twenty-eight years old, some might say I'm a bit young to write an autobiography.

However, this is very much my 'story so far', in my own words, as to how I've carved out a career in country music, a career that stemmed from true graft and hard work in pubs and clubs in England as a very young teenage boy and which has developed and grown across the Irish Sea, where I returned to my family's roots and became a household name, playing arena shows in Ireland's biggest venues.

For many years now I've had the pleasure of performing not only in Ireland but all over the UK, in places like my home town of Liverpool and at the London Palladium – I've even trodden the boards of the Grand Ole Opry in Nashville, which really was a dream come true for me.

I'm often asked about how it all happened and where it all began, so I decided to write this book, not only to tell of my path to performing on some of the world's most famous stages, but also to give those who have followed me from my early days a glimpse into what life is like for me behind the scenes when I take to the road on my tours with the band and what I do to relax during my – very rare – days off. I hope these words let you get to know me a little bit better and, for those of you who also dream of a life on the road, like I always have, maybe you can pick up some tips from my experiences.

I hope you enjoy learning about some of my adventures – and a few good old misadventures – along the way. This book is a small token of my appreciation for everyone who has helped me get this far, and I'd like to sincerely thank each and every one of you for helping me live out my dream.

I'll see you on the road very soon. Until then, take care.

Love, Nathan x

Prologue: Born for the Road

Tuesday, 23 January 2018: Two days before the UK Livin'
the Dream *tour, Enniskillen, County Fermanagh*

At long last, after three weeks that have felt like forever, it's finally time to get back on the road again.

Following a lengthy Christmas break from gigging, I'm rounding up the lads once more to do what we do best – getting on the stage and playing some music – and with a four-week-long UK tour ahead of us, topped off by two arena gigs on Ireland's biggest stages, the 3Arena Dublin and the SSE in Belfast, plus a trip to America, where we'll join a Caribbean cruise with artists including Engelbert Humperdinck, Charlie Pride and The High Kings (and lots of sunshine, of course!), plus a weekend at the Hilton in Blackpool, we are mad to dust off the winter hibernation and get stuck in.

I wake up after a restless night around 7.45 a.m. and my head is buzzing with ideas for songs, rehearsals and all that has still to be done before we go across to England to kick off the *Livin' the Dream* tour. I never sleep well before going on the road; I suppose it's a mixture of adrenaline and excitement, like a spark that lights up inside me when I'm planning to do what I truly love, but the good news is that the snowy Fermanagh countryside has finally thawed and the sun has come out, just in time to see us off on our travels.

This week marks eight years since I formed my first band here in Ireland and as I load up the jeep with the sound desk and PA I need for today's rehearsals I take a moment to reflect on how much has changed since I made the big move to relocate here and follow my dream of being a full-time performer.

I've stood on some of the UK and Ireland's biggest stages, where I've entertained thousands; I've sung with people I long admired growing up as a young boy in Liverpool; and I've shared the spotlight with superstars that I'd only ever have dreamed of meeting.

I've recorded nine studio albums, six live albums, hosted my own TV show on RTÉ, had my on-screen acting debut in Irish soap opera *Ros na Rún*, received numerous awards along the way, and the best thing of all is that I get to work with some of my favourite people in the music industry on a daily basis. Now I'm pumped to get out there and do it all again.

But first, it's rehearsal day and I'm excited to get started. There's so much to do before we head for Billingham, where we'll kick off the tour just two days from now, and my first stop this morning will be in Sligo, where I'm going to get kitted out in new clothes for both on- and off-stage. I grab some breakfast on the go at the twenty-four-hour service station (an apple and two bottles of water) and set off to see what Tommy Clarke at EJ Menswear in Sligo has in mind for me to wear on this trip.

I'm so lucky to be supported by local businesses who help me do what I do in the best way, and that includes making sure I look the part, so after trying on seven or eight outfits at EJ Menswear, who have looked after both me and the band for special occasions for the past three years, Tommy has me sorted. I have a formal outfit (a suit jacket, waistcoat and tie) and a casual jacket with jeans and a T-shirt, all of which will come in very handy both when I'm performing and when I'm not.

Next stop is my accountant, who keeps me right when it comes to the business end of things and, with the end of the financial year looming, while it might not be my favourite element of the job, it's important to keep on top of it. Running a band and all that goes with it has a huge financial element to it, and it's up to me and my manager, John Farry, to make sure that everything this end is in proper order. We have running costs, transport and travel expenses when on the road; there are the wages for the band and the crew, outlays on the PA and equipment, on production, like lighting and sound, and then there's the merchandise, not to mention ticket and music sales, video production, photography and branding – we have to keep on top of them all. Whoever thought it was all only about singing!!

With this formality out of the way, I set off for the Kilmore Hotel in Cavan, where I'll meet up with my band – Gareth Lowry (drums), John Byrne (sax, piano and whistles), John Pettifer (lead guitar), Tom Sheerin (fiddle), Matthew Curran (guitar, harmonica, banjo and backing vocals) and Carl Harvey (bass guitar/double-bass). We're good buddies by now and, after not seeing them all together since before Christmas, I'm really looking forward to making some music and having the craic with them all again. It's a bit of a cliché, but we are all like a family when we travel together and, when I pull up at the hotel, I can tell that everyone is in good form and raring to go.

The Kilmore Hotel is a good meeting point for today as it's almost a halfway mark for us all and, without our crew to get us set up, we lift the gear from the jeep, Gareth sets up the drums and the others set up guitars, keyboards and microphones, and we're soon ready to go over our set list for our gigs in England and Wales over the next four weeks. We'll visit towns and cities including Telford, Billingham,

Carlisle (we've sold out there for the first time, which is cool), my home town of Liverpool, as well as Manchester, Dunstable, Cardiff, Birmingham, Chatham, Barnstaple, Hayes, Nottingham, Christchurch, London and Clacton-on-Sea.

With seven new songs to learn and a brand-new acoustic set for the first time, which I'm really looking forward to, we gather round in a circle and waste no time in getting started. The acoustic set will lend a new feel to our set, and we've chosen three songs – the Richard Thompson folk classic 'Beeswing', Alison Krauss's version of 'When You Say Nothing at All' and the good old favourite 'Cecilia' by Simon and Garfunkel. The boys will take up new positions on stage for this part of the show, with Carl swapping his bass guitar for a double bass, Tom will play the fiddle and mandolin, while Matt and John will take up acoustic guitars. We're aiming for a bluegrass sound and, before long, it begins to take shape.

There's a lot to prepare for as well as set lists before we go on the road, and Derek Reilly, who drives the truck, operates the lights and fixes up the instruments when needs be is my go-to man for production ideas. We've repositioned everyone onstage this time, and I've invested in a new velvet backdrop, which should lend a nice feel to the onstage appearance, as well as some nice dark blue velvet jackets for the lads. As we run through the songs, I'm delighted that everyone has lots of ideas on how they should sound, and we come up with a new intro for the show. It's all coming together, and I feel the rush of progress, which always reminds me why I love this job so much.

I work best under pressure, so I like to leave it to the last minute to decide on what songs come first, and then it's over to Derek to tie up the lighting ideas and James Enevoldson on sound to work on the running order we've chosen and help bring the show to life.

By six o'clock, and with only two tea breaks in between, I can feel the hunger set in, but I've no time for food just yet. We pack up the gear, and the lads set off home while Derek and I hang back in the hotel foyer to meet up with Ciara Davey, a production designer who we've hired in to look after the big arena shows in Belfast and Dublin at the end of March. We talk lighting designs, sound effects and costumes, and it's a fairly intensely packed discussion, as we won't see Ciara again until after the UK tour. The time flies by, despite my tummy rumbling, and before long it's 10.30 p.m. and I'm finally on the road home.

I stop off and grab a wrap at the twenty-four-hour filling station and eat it on the way home, happy in my thoughts as to how the day has gone, not to mention finally having some food! I love being productive, it really fires me up, but it's time to switch off for the night and, after checking in with social media, I get into bed, ready and looking forward to another busy day ahead.

Wednesday, 24 January 2018: One day before the UK Livin' the Dream tour

This morning we've a lot to pack in, so once again, bright and early, John Pettifer (or JP, as he is fondly known), Gareth and I set off for Belfast, bound for the UTV studios on the Ormeau Road, where we'll meet up with bass player Carl to record a section of a UTV *Life* special which will air this Friday night. The UTV crew and the show's roving reporter Ruth Fitzgerald have already been in Liverpool, where they met and interviewed my family, and they have collected a montage of clips of my home town and some of the places that featured in my childhood, so it should be a nice piece when it's all put together. I watch the VT and see them visit the Irish Centre, where I used to play music when I was just a boy. Ruth also spoke to some of my early teachers; plus, my mum and grandparents got the chance to show off some very embarrassing photos of my childhood days! It feels very nostalgic to watch my mum onscreen talking about me in such an endearing way. She tells Ruth that when I'm back home with her and my dad, I lie up on the sofa and watch TV like any normal family member does, and I have to say that's the truth. I love getting home to Liverpool as often as my schedule allows, and seeing my mum on the VT makes me excited that I'll be seeing her when I play the Philharmonic Hall in just a couple of days' time.

Back in the Belfast studio, though, it's time to get our mics on and get ready for action. Today, I will be interviewed by the programme's host, Pamela Ballantine, who always has a friendly welcome for us all when we visit UTV, and after a bit of a chat on air about the forthcoming arena gigs in Belfast and Dublin I get the chance to sing a song I love called 'Liverpool', and my brand-new song, a single I've recorded called 'This Song is for You' for Valentine's Day. It's a beautiful ballad about never-ending love – and who doesn't like a bit of romance on Valentine's Day!

The interview is fun and relaxed, and I'm very honoured that the production team at UTV *Life* have dedicated a full show to me and my life growing up in Liverpool. The support I get from both the Irish and the UK media is something I will never take for granted, and watching the footage from my parents' home and seeing some old faces from my past was very touching and enjoyable, even if Mum did dig deep into the family album and show those photos I'd rather keep in the archives!

We finish off with Pamela and the UTV crew around

lunchtime, and I stick with the new Valentine's song release theme for another while, as it's time to make a video to match the song. I take a two-hour journey to Kells in County Meath, where I'll meet up with an amazingly talented and very cool director called Ovie, who I worked with before on several other music videos, including 'Summer's Here' just under a year ago. Ovie is from Dublin, and I love his eye for creativity and how he can bring magic to my music videos with his energy and ideas. In fact, today's location was his idea, and I'm truly blown away when we arrive at Headfort House, a sprawling estate in the Kells countryside and home to a junior boarding school – one of very few left in the country. Our exact location is the grand ballroom within the house, which is totally breathtaking in every way. Over two hundred years old, it was designed by renowned architect George Semple for the Earl of Bective, and it's just perfect for the performance element of my new video, which will feature me playing a grand piano in the centre of the room in an interior designed by Scottish architect Robert Adam. The ceilings are high with panelled walls and chimneypieces sculpted in white marble, and huge portraits of members of the Headfort family look down at us as we make some minor adjustments to the room to suit our shoot. As this building is so precious and still includes some furniture selected by Adam, we have to be very careful when moving things and there are strict stipulations as to what we can and cannot do, but Ovie has some fantastic ideas and, before long, the cameras are rolling and the video comes to life.

We take the old piano lid off to expose the inside mechanics, which really adds to the authentic feel, and I'm delighted when Ovie says, just a couple of hours later, he's happy with what we've got. His new footage at Headfort House will fit in perfectly with the rest of the video, which shows an old couple looking through photos of their life on a projector and tells the story of their lengthy romance. I can't wait to see the finished product when Ovie puts it all together.

Happy with our progress, I say my farewells to Ovie and all at Headfort House and set off home for Fermanagh, pleased again to have packed in as much as I can before we hit the road tomorrow. I do two radio interviews on the phone when I get home – one with a Manchester station and one with a Liverpool station – to promote the weekend gigs over there, and then I hit the sack, my head once again racing with plans for all that we have prepared for as the big day comes round. I should sleep tonight – restlessly again, maybe – but I'm tired enough to nod off and, as it's my last night for a while in my own bed, I'm going to try and make the most of it.

My sleeping quarters for the best part of the next few weeks will be in a tiny bunkbed on our tour bus as we travel the length and breadth of England and Wales, but it's a fun environment and everyone spends a lot of time on their phones as we travel, watching Netflix or catching up with friends and family (we all have a little charger station by our bed). The bus sleeps fourteen people, which includes our crew, the band, me and my nan, who is in charge of merchandising, among other things, and at night we'll play cards to unwind after a gig and have a laugh together.

We'll fly out on the first flight to Newcastle in the morning, where we'll meet Derek, who will have sailed ahead of us with the truck from Dublin to Holyhead, and it's all systems go until we reach our first venue, the Billingham Forum Theatre, which is about a forty-minute drive from the airport.

It's going to be a crazy few weeks and I'm really looking forward to it, with my gig in Liverpool and St Patrick's Night at the London Palladium two places in particular that I can't wait to perform in. It's always a huge honour to play my home town, as I get to see some familiar faces, and I've put together a very lengthy guest list for that gig, which includes my immediate family and cousins, of course, plus my dad's best man, my mum's best friend and some of my old friends from my early days playing music around the bars in Liverpool, and I'm looking forward to seeing some good schoolfriends who, nowadays, I don't get to see as often as I'd like to. My grandad, John McCoy, or Grumps, as he is fondly known, might even join me for a song on the evening, but I'll have to twist his arm a bit to get him to come up on stage (or will I?!). At eighty-four years old, Grumps still really does enjoy performing his party piece – but I'll save that story until I see if he is up for it on the night!

As well as my Liverpool gig, performing at the London Palladium is just something else, and I get butterflies just thinking of returning there. It's a truly iconic venue that has hosted stars such as Frank Sinatra, whose picture looks down on you in the dressing room, which is very surreal, plus Jerry Lee Lewis, Dean Martin, Diana Ross, Sammy Davis Jr, Gypsy Rose Lee, Shirley Bassey, Nat King Cole and my fellow Merseyside music men The Beatles, whose appearance there on 13 October 1963 led to the coining of the phrase 'Beatlemania', due to the scenes of screaming fans. I sometimes really have to pinch myself when I think that I will be playing such a celebrated stage again on St Patrick's Night, 17 March, an occasion that already means so much to me because of my family's Irish roots and my love of Irish music.

As I drift off to sleep, I'm genuinely humbled, and so thankful that I get to do what I really love for a living and all that the past twelve years or so has brought my way. Being on the road is where I feel most comfortable, where I can really be myself, and I totally believe that it's what I was meant to do. All my life I knew it. Ever since I picked up my first accordion as a little boy I wanted to be a performer and now, here I am, getting to live out my dream every day.

Morning comes in what seems like the blink of an eye and I smile as I realize it's almost showtime.

It's 5 a.m., I'm extremely tired after a very busy few days, but I'm also ready and up for the challenge and I can't wait to get out there and sing my new songs.

I was meant to do this. I was born for the road.

PART ONE
My Story So Far

1. Monday's Child

After a very long evening in the labour ward at Oxford Maternity Hospital in Liverpool, at 12.50 a.m. on my due date of Monday, 28 May 1990, my mother, Noreen, gave birth to me by emergency caesarean section and I was named Nathan Kane Tyrone Anthony Carter weighing a whole big . . . well, maybe not so big, 6lb 5oz.

It was never either of my parents' intention to give me so many first names but, as I was the first grandson on the maternal side of my family and because my mum was one of three sisters, to have a boy was quite a surprise to them all, so it seems that everyone, even the priest, had to have their say.

Mum wanted to call me Nathan, a Hebrew name which means 'he gave' or 'God's gift', and after all she had been through it seems pretty fair that she got first choice. Dad was second in line with Kane, an Irish name meaning 'little battler', and my grandad 'Grumps' John McCoy (my mum's father) was a big fan of the actor Tyrone Power, so he had to make sure he had a name in there too.

Nathan Kane Tyrone . . . three names were plenty, or so it would have seemed, but it was only when they all arrived a few weeks later to christen me at Bishop Eton Catholic church that they were told they needed to add in a saint's name too, and so on the spot they chose the name of the priest, Father Anthony Hodgett, and there I was, fully named and ready to take on the world, four names and all! If that wasn't enough, in later years, when I made my Confirmation, I had the name John thrown into the mix as well!

I was born in the year of the Horse, and if you follow the Chinese zodiac, this apparently makes me open-minded, flexible, honest and extremely energetic, all of which I hope is very true, of course. As a Gemini, I was destined to be quick-witted, restless, sociable and ready for fun. Margaret Thatcher was coming to the end of her term as British prime minister back then, and the more popular songs of the times were Madonna's 'Vogue' and Elton John's 'Sacrifice'. The Gulf War crisis was at its peak, Nelson Mandela was freed from prison in South Africa and the whole world was getting ready for a summer of football as Italia '90 fever brewed throughout our streets, towns, villages and cities.

My parents, Ian and Noreen Carter, lived at 86 Woolton Road, a semi-detached, three-bedroom house in the suburbs of Liverpool, and the evening before I was born they were at a wedding, when I interrupted the celebrations by deciding I was ready for action – or not, so it seemed, as they were sent home again, only to return to the hospital later that evening, when I was well and truly on the way second time around.

My mum tells me that she had an enjoyable pregnancy, and that during it she craved tomatoes (which I, incidentally, can't stand), she totally went off the very smell of alcohol (which I, incidentally, *can* stand) and she enjoyed a box or ten of Maltesers, which she most definitely would never share with anyone.

The midwife who was on duty that night stayed on after her shift, as she'd seen my mum through most of her labour, and Dad almost missed the big moment, all in the name of fetching a newspaper! When I was taking a bit too long to make my grand appearance, Mum was being prepped for theatre and Dad nipped out, but when he returned they'd already wheeled Mum into theatre and it was a rush to have him gowned up and into the room. He only just made it in time!

When the doctor announced that Mum had given birth to a baby boy, Mum couldn't believe it. She'd been convinced she'd be having a girl.

Dad told my nan (Ann McCoy) that she had a grandchild, and Nan's first reaction was similar, as she asked, 'What's she like?', assuming too that I'd be a girl, as she'd had three girls herself, so I think it's fair to say that I was a bit of a surprise to that side of the family, hence the excitement and the numerous names I was given by them all!

I was brought home to Woolton Road on 2 June. All four of my grandparents were there to greet me, and they had flowers waiting for Mum and had set up the crib for our grand arrival. My dad's parents, John and Amana Carter, were known as Nana and Grandad, and they were as proud as punch of their new grandson. They were a marvellous couple and they have such an interesting story as to how they met, which I love to tell. John Carter was a builder from Liverpool who was working for a very wealthy Arabian man, and he fell in love with the boss's daughter, the very beautiful Amana. When Amana's parents told her to choose between life with the humble Merseyside brickie or life as she knew it (which probably would have meant an arranged marriage), she chose love and ran away with John, staying with his parents until her own family came round to the idea – eventually. It did take a long time. The rest is history, as they went on to be happily married and have seven children together. She remained very close to her family, thank goodness, and I sometimes think this might be where my brother and sister get their dark skin from, but somehow I missed out on that gene, as I got the paler Irish skin tone!

That Irish look comes, of course, from my maternal grandmother, Ann, or Nan, as I've always known her, and it's a name that most of my fans fondly call her by now. Nan's mum was Winifred Ward (Winnie), and she was from Warrenpoint in County Down, a seaside town near Newry. The Ward family decided to emigrate to America, but when they got to Liverpool they ended up staying, and that was where Winnie met James O'Neill from County Cork. They married, and my nan was one of their children.

Nan later met John McCoy (Grumps), a purser who worked for the Merchant Navy and, together, they had three daughters: Oona, Siobhan and my mother, Noreen.

My mum remembers a newspaper announcement around the time of my birth which read 'The Gift of a Precious Son' and how my great-aunt, another Noreen, came from London to stay with us for a week to help her out with looking after me and by doing some night feeds, which was fantastic for Mum after her C-section, as Dad had to go back to work. Great-aunt Noreen was 'great' at many things, including controlling visitors: she was very much a believer that Mum and baby needed to rest and she chased a few away who called at times she deemed unsuitable!

I'm told I was a very well-behaved baby and I'd love the usual bath, bottle, cuddle and then bed. I'd go to sleep without any fuss ... yes, I'd go straight to sleep and I'd sleep sound until just a few hours later, at 2 a.m., when I'd wake up bright as a button and ready to get up to face the day ahead! My poor parents, who were then both back at work – my dad straight away as a building contractor and my mum, who returned to her job as a housing officer in the City Council when I was five months old – had to take turns to get up and entertain me until morning, which mainly entailed letting me watch TV or keeping me busy with toys and stories.

As a young baby I loved all the usual television programmes, like *Barney the Dinosaur, Come Outside, Rosie and Jim, Sesame Street* and all the Disney movies, but I hated cartoons.

I knew all the words to an American song called 'Baby Beluga in the Deep Blue Sea' as soon as I was old enough to talk. In fact, the midwife who helped deliver me in hospital said I was born singing, so maybe I knew what I wanted to do – sing and stay up all night – from the very moment I was born!

My first word was 'Dada' when I was seven months old, but when I started to walk it was my mum who I took eight steps towards, just a week before my first birthday, and I've always said I could never choose to be either a mummy or a daddy's boy, so it looks like I was even with them from a very young age and showed no favouritism whatsoever.

Like most young toddlers, I was prone to the odd accident and, when my mum's cousin Sara came round to trim my hair when I was about two years old, I decided I'd had enough and jumped up off the chair, had a run-in with the scissors and cut my head quite badly. I had to be taken to hospital to have stitches. My poor dad got quite a shock when he came home from work, only to see the kitchen covered in blood and no sign of either myself or my mum. Thank goodness we all have mobile phones now, to avoid any such panic!

I loved noise and was known to carry around a little Fisher-Price toy microphone and cassette recorder, which I'd sing into from a very young age. This soon progressed to a toy piano, and my mum's friend Margaret bought me a tiny little concertina, like the ones the TV characters Rosie and Jim have, for my first birthday in 1991, which I made sure everyone heard me playing at every given opportunity. My long-suffering, sleep-deprived parents avoided any noisy presents on that occasion and instead got me a swing for the garden and a new bike – maybe they were trying to really tire me out by making sure I got plenty of fresh air during the day now that I was up on my feet walking, though it obviously didn't work, as I kept up my non-sleeping patterns for another few years. No wonder there was a six-year gap between me and my sister!

In order to give my mum a bit of a break, my nan, who always lived in the same area as we did, would come and take me out for a few hours, and Grumps would try to sing me to sleep with his favourite country songs by artists such as Johnny Cash, Dolly Parton and Willie Nelson. By the age of two, I knew all the words to Grumps' favourite song of all time and his party piece to this day, Elvis Presley's 'Are You Lonesome Tonight?', so as far as musical taste was concerned, I was in safe hands from very early on. At home, Mum and Dad loved to listen to Simply Red, Lionel Richie and anything Motown, so I always had variety, but it was country and Irish music that really caught my ear even back then.

I spent a lot of time as a very young child with Nan and Grumps, and I'd constantly be surrounded by their choice of music, be it on their radio at home, on the telly on their VHS and, later, on their extensive DVD collection or in the social club where Nan worked and where she ran many live music events. Mind you, Nan wasn't one for actually babysitting me at home – she couldn't stay in the one place for long enough – so when Mum and Dad fancied an evening out or even just when they went shopping, Mum's aunt Bernie would look after me and would stay overnight to let them have some time out.

Despite Grumps' attempts at singing me to sleep, and despite being an angelic child during the day, me not sleeping at night didn't show any sign of waning until I started school at the age of four. I can only imagine how delighted my parents must have been to have finally been able to have a proper night's sleep. I'm told that I slept only one full night, from 10.30 p.m. until six in the morning, for four whole years and, as much as I'm used to late nights nowadays, I have to say I feel sorry for them having been so deprived of sleep when I was so young and they both worked so hard.

It was at this same age of four, just a few months after I started school, that I was gifted a musical instrument of a more proper variety from Santa Claus. My love of noise and making sounds was showing no signs of ever going away, and I knew exactly what it was I wanted.

I'd spent those earliest years of my life in awe of musicians, especially Ronnie Kennedy, a white-haired man from Daniel O'Donnell's band who played the accordion, so when I was taken to the toy store to get some ideas for my Christmas list and saw a similar-looking white-haired man there I had a light-bulb moment as to what I wanted from Santa.

I didn't want toys, oh no. I'd had enough of swings and bikes and Rosie and Jim by then, so that Christmas, having remembered the tiny concertina I had as a baby, I asked for my very first proper accordion, and a new way of making proper sounds and, very soon, real music, was just about to begin.

2. Early Memories and First Tunes

I'm not sure who cried the most on my first day at school, but it was a tight competition between my mum and me when I first set foot in Bishop Eton Primary School. There I was, decked out in my new uniform of grey shorts, a white shirt, green-and-yellow tie, green jumper, grey socks and black shoes, bawling my eyes out as I watched my mother leave me, crying her own heart out too.

I don't know why I was so overwhelmed by my first day there, as I'd been in full-time nursery since I was a baby, so it wasn't that I was used to being at home with Mum all the time. I do recall how I'd spent a lot of time during my play-group year daydreaming of being onstage, so maybe I was just a bit put out that I was going to have to go through all of this education process first before I could start playing music, which is what I really wanted to do, like the singers I watched on television all the time.

As soon as I could hold my new piano accordion that Santa had dutifully delivered for Christmas that year, I was trying to play tunes, and I used to put out chairs in Nan's lounge and make little paper tickets for my aunties and uncles to be my 'audience'. I knew every word by then of all of Daniel O'Donnell's songs, and I used to copy what Daniel would have worn back then, especially a groovy cream jacket that I really liked, and I'd play and sing my heart out for the poor folk who were forced to sit through it.

'Was I good, Nan?' I'd ask after my 'performance'.

'Nah,' she'd reply playfully. 'You'd need to keep practising.'

And practise I did, led by my grandad John Carter, who taught me my first two tunes, the popular ballads 'Danny Boy' and 'Black Velvet Band'.

As well as being taught by Grandad John, I'd spend hours and hours with Nan at the Parish Centre, a social club where she worked, and I'd watch the bands who entertained there come and go, and she'd also take me to the Liverpool Irish Centre, where I learned to play the tin whistle. The Liverpool Irish Centre was a real hub for ex-pats to gather and listen to folk songs and take part in other cultural activities, like music lessons and céilí dances, and my great-aunt Bernie and her friend Patricia Murphy, who we knew as Pat, would often take me there on a Sunday afternoon, and Bernie would sing to me a song called 'Underneath the Lamplight'.

The Irish Centre was located in the city centre, and it was a very old, listed building that could hold up to seven hundred people at a time, so you can imagine how, as a tiny little boy, it seemed absolutely huge to me back then. Every Sunday we'd go there to hear different singers, and I remember being in awe of a man called Sean Wilson, from Toomebridge in County Antrim, who played the accordion and would belt out tunes like 'Wild Rover' and 'The Fields of Athenry'. I wanted to be able to do that so badly.

I just adored the sound of the accordion, with its strong, bellowing, free sounds, and when Sean would finish his set, another guy called Michael Coyne would take to the stage, and again I would stand there watching, open-mouthed and taking it all in, hoping that one day I would be able to play the same tunes as well as they could.

By the time I was six or seven my parents recognized that I needed some proper lessons on both the accordion and the piano, and I had three very influential teachers throughout my childhood.

Polly Beck was a classically trained singing teacher who put me through all my grades when I was at primary school. I began my lessons at her own house but, as she had two young children to look after, it soon became more practical if she came to our house, and Mum would watch her wee ones as they played and make us all some food for the end of the lesson. Polly soon became a close family friend and I was very lucky to have lessons from her. She taught me so much.

From around the same age, Kathleen Hudson taught me piano at her home, which was about five minutes away from where we lived. Kathleen was in her seventies and could be quite strict with me when she wanted to be, but she was also a great teacher and when I would grasp the tunes she was teaching me she would reward me with sweets, which, of course, I never refused. She taught me traditional jigs such as 'The Irish Washerwoman', which is very well known and dates back to at least 1715, and the 'Kerry Polka', or 'Egan's Polka', which is an upbeat dance-along tune and very popular with young learners. The lessons would normally end when Grumps came to pick me up but, instead of going straight home, we'd stay there for another half-hour or so while he sang songs along to Kathleen's piano-playing. Kathleen was a great character and, even though I said she was strict, she probably let me get away with murder when it came to learning. I always enjoyed going to her house for lessons, as well as seeing her when she came to visit us, as she always brought a lot of joy when she called, not to mention a sing-song or two. Her grandson Patrick Needham was my best friend at the time, and Patrick's dad, Steve, also played music, so it was a lovely atmosphere to be around. I stayed with Kathleen for lessons until she passed away, and there was a great emptiness for a long time when she left us, but her music and legacy lived on.

In my early teens, after Kathleen's passing, my piano and accordion teacher was an Irish lady called Geraldine Lynch who played in a band called The Four Counties. Geraldine is one of the nicest people I've ever met and we are still great friends to this day.

The Liverpool Branch of Comhaltas (pronounced *koh-al-tas*) was another outlet for my very early music lessons. Comhaltas is a group of people from an area who promote Irish culture, mainly through music and dancing, and the Liverpool branch was one of the finest in Britain. Comhaltas hosted weekly music lessons in all sorts of instruments and monthly music 'sessions' where all the students and more established musicians from traditional Irish backgrounds would gather and play music together. A sea of fiddles, accordions, bodhráns (an Irish drum), whistles, banjos, mandolins and the finest of ballad singers would meet up at the Irish Centre once a month, and it was the perfect environment for a budding musician like me to learn my way and practise performing in front of a ready-made audience.

'Was I good, Nan?' I'd ask after the Comhaltas, just like I used to when I'd do my mini-concerts at her house a few years before.

'You're getting better,' she'd tell me with a smile. 'Keep practising.'

And so I did keep practising, and I'd grasp every opportunity to learn more and more from anyone who came my way.

One of those people was Gary Lynch, a fantastic young fiddle player who was part of Comhaltas and who hailed from Roslea in County Fermanagh. Gary came to Liverpool to study at university and so, to earn a few extra pounds, he ended up waiting in the bar of the social club where Nan was in charge and he stayed around for about three or four years and passed a lot of his musical knowledge on to my eager-to-learn ears. Gary was very easy-going and always up for the craic and, even though he now lives in Dublin and I don't get to see him very often, we still do keep in touch – that's one of the greatest things about music. You get to meet so many people, and I've been so lucky to have built up a wide circle of not only talented musicians but those I can genuinely call my friends.

Outside of the music world, I had other friends too of course, and one of my best buddies back then was called Matthew, or Mattie, Thompson, who went to the same school and lived just a mile or so up the road from me. We used to spend every spare hour we had riding our bikes down to the Pier Head or around the nearby park and, when I was six years old, my dad bought me a little motorbike, which was very exciting for two adventurous kids like Mattie and me. Every weekend Dad would take me and a friend out to empty fields with the motorbike and we'd build ramps out of car bonnets and have a whale of a time scrambling over every type of hurdle we could make for ourselves. One day we were joined by another friend, Nicholas, who was eager to have his turn on the bike. Before he set off, Dad asked Nicholas if he knew what to do.

'I do,' said Nicholas, which of course was a little white lie. When he disappeared off into the distance and still hadn't come back almost five minutes later, we followed his path to find him covered in red and pinned into a bush with my precious bike upside down next to him. The first thing I asked was if my bike was okay (it was!), but poor Nicholas wasn't and he arrived into school the next day in a sling, with his arm fractured in two places. My dad of course was absolutely mortified, though, thankfully, the red that Nicholas was covered in wasn't blood but berries from the bush he crashed into! Nonetheless, his accident put an end to my carefree biking days, much to my despair, and the bike was sold.

Along with friends such as Mattie and Nicholas, I made my First Holy Communion when I was seven years old. First Holy Communion is a big event in Catholic school life and I was lucky enough to have had a big party on the lawn of the Parish Centre, where all my family gathered to mark the occasion. As I was the first grandchild to make my Communion, there were a lot of aunties, uncles and cousins in attendance, and we had bouncy castles, lots of food and I got plenty of money (what every child really wants on the Communion Day!) and a pile of holy gifts which are probably still in their boxes! Like most people, the photos from my Communion are far from fashionable nowadays and, in my photos, I am rocking a mop of fairish brown hair which was cut into the shape of a bowl and wearing a white shirt and a red tie with grey socks and grey shorts, all topped off by an obligatory crucifix round my neck.

Making First Holy Communion is one of the more stand-out occasions that I remember from my early school days, but I have to admit I never really did like school at all. I pulled sickies at least ten times during my time there and I recall vividly how, one day, I pretended to throw up and even faked a throbbing headache, knowing fine well that Nan, who worked right next door at the Parish Centre, would be able to come and get me without disturbing my parents, who would be at their own jobs a bit further into town.

On this particular day, as Nan and I left the school, my illness having, as always, automatically vanished as soon as I hit the fresh air of freedom, my heart stopped when I saw the police outside the Parish Centre. I was sure they were there to get me and had caught on to my repeat-offender habits of pretending I was sick to get out of class early. To my absolute relief, they were in fact there to investigate a burglary at the Parish Centre, so a whole unexpected afternoon of drama came my way, which was much more exciting to me than being stuck at school!

I did enjoy some subjects, of course, and I loved learning recorder and taking part in the primary school choir when I was little. I enjoyed maths too, but escaping to the Parish Centre was always much more fun, even though it probably didn't happen as often as I think it did.

Despite not being too fussed about the whole academic side of school life, I do have nice memories of some teachers, like Miss Baker, who was very kind to me and who I still see from time to time when she turns up for my gigs. Even though choir was my favourite part of those primary-school days at Bishop Eton, I was sent to the headmaster on a few occasions by the music teacher, Mrs Aston, who always seemed to catch me out for talking or not paying attention. She was incredibly strict and shouted a lot, and I used to think she might have had a pick on me, but it didn't put me off and I loved singing my heart out in the choir on every occasion. I also remember the sadness surrounding the very premature death of Miss Bird, who was only in her late twenties when she passed away suddenly from a brain aneurysm. It was a huge shock to the entire school community, and it puzzled me as to how someone so pleasant and so young could have been taken from this world so soon.

Taking part in the choir presented lots of opportunities and we really were so lucky to have had such forward-thinking teachers – they were well ahead of their time. Every year they would arrange a great Christmas concert for us to take part in and, one year, when I was about nine years old, I got to perform at the Philharmonic Hall with Gerry Marsden. We sang 'Ferry 'Cross the Mersey' and 'You'll Never Walk Alone', which was a big honour and very exciting for such a young school choir to be part of.

It was around the same age or so that I also discovered CDs and pop music, and the very first CD I bought was none other than the Spice Girls, who were at the peak of their career in the late nineties. I was taken to the cinema to see their movie *Spice World* with some cousins and, afterwards, we couldn't wait to get to Woolworths to buy their latest single 'Stop', which was a big hit that we all loved. I became totally convinced that I was going to one day marry 'Baby Spice' Emma Bunton, which of course hasn't happened (yet!), but you never know ... actually, I think I've missed the boat on that one!

Speaking of early crushes, another highlight of primary school was a girl called Charlotte Woodward who I fell madly in love with when I was nine or ten years old. Charlotte had the most beautiful long red hair, and my friends set us up to meet at Calderstones Park. It was there that I experienced my very first kiss, a rushed, nervous event, as most first kisses are (especially when you're only nine!), but one that I will always remember fondly, even though I never did see her again after primary school.

Looking back on those early days, I have to say that my childhood really was enriched in so many ways and I'm so very lucky to be able to look back on so many fond memories of a happy home and days and nights filled with songs and tunes, plus a hunger for learning what I loved to do best, all of which was nurtured so closely by my wonderful family.

3. My Family

My days of being an only child ended when I was six, with the birth of my sister, Kiara, in December 1996, and then my brother was born less than two years later, in August 1998 – Jacob, or Jake, as he is now better known. My mum always jokes that it took her all that time to get over me not sleeping for her to take on another baby, but I was thrilled to bits when I finally became a big brother.

I took to my new role of big brother like a duck to water and I loved to help out, fetching things for Mum when she needed a hand. Jake and Kiara looked very much like my dad and his side of the family and they brought a new energy and a lot of noise to our family – all in the best possible way, of course!

I had always been a quiet and reserved child, and the most noise I made was when I was playing my accordion or piano, but these two little balls of fire brought a very different way of life and I loved every minute of it, and even though each of us have very different personalities and different tastes, I have to say we all got along together . . . most of the time!

The three of us loved the outdoors as children and Mum and Dad would take us to the local Calderstones Park, where we'd ride our bikes, feed the ducks and go to the café for a bite to eat on the way home. Our house was always busy, with friends coming and going, and since my dad is the youngest of a big family, we had loads of cousins in and out all the time. Nan and Grumps McCoy were often around, as they lived nearby, and we also loved visiting our grandparents on the Carter side at Christmas, especially as my grandmother Amana's house was like our very own grotto. She'd decorate it from top to bottom, and it was paradise for so many grandchildren and great-grandchildren to run around, and every year she'd throw a big party for us all, which was always great fun. I think we were special to her because we were her youngest grandchildren, and she really was hands on, playing board games, cards and bingo with us, plus she always bought us very big and very noisy presents, which I'm sure my parents dreaded to see her coming with!

Growing up, we had no phones or iPads of course, but we loved watching telly and we were pretty good at sharing toys and just muddled in together. Kiara was very much a tomboy, but she loved dolls – she is the rebel of the family; Jake jokes that, if you asked her to get you a glass of milk, she'd come back with a glass of Lucozade, just to be different! Jake is the cheeky chappie of the house and what you see is what you get. He is always honest and always has an answer for everything, whereas Kiara and I are more apologetic and aim to please – though he would argue his point until the bitter end!

I absolutely loved being a big brother, despite the age gap, and Jake and Kiara soon found the Irish Centre to be a big part of their lives too, and they'd come to watch me play music there, soon taking up their own instruments, with Jake playing the fiddle and singing while Kiara also sang and played concertina, the tin whistle and piano.

Jake was always the typical annoying little brother, wanting to go everywhere with me, and I often had to look out for him. As we've got older, the eight-year age gap seems to have lessened and we really are very close now, but when he was very young I do recall one prank that Kiara and I played on him which might have scarred him emotionally for life . . .

We were playing in Jake's bedroom – he was probably about three years old at the time – and when he left the room Kiara and I hid in his wardrobe. When he came back in, he couldn't find us, and eventually we pounced out of the wardrobe, totally petrifying the poor child. For almost a year later, he wouldn't sleep on his own, as he was so afraid of what might jump out on him!

Our childhood was made up of playing football, cricket and rounders in the garden, bouncing on trampolines and playing 'Piley On' outside, which once ended up in a hospital visit, when I broke my arm and elbow (and Jake managed to knock himself out during some horseplay also) – so just typical behaviour of kids our age! My birthday parties were always in the garden and I loved a slice of Billy Bear ham and milk roll to celebrate the years going by.

Nowadays, Kiara and I have stopped scaring people unexpectedly, you'll be glad to know – much to Jake's relief also! I keep in touch with her as much as I can, and I try and pass on some big-brotherly advice when she might need it, but she is very much her own person and prefers to do her own thing. She's a great girl and gets on with anyone of any age (she's a bit like me in that way, I suppose), and I sometimes think that she listens a bit more to me than she does our parents, which is probably typical of most siblings.

When Jake and I get together now we are a bit like the characters in *Dumb and Dumber*, always messing and always laughing, and I try and embarrass him by telling him how much he loves himself. I joke that, if he was chocolate, he would eat himself! We had many laugh-out-loud moments growing up, but I do recall one incident when the smile was on the other side of my face . . .

I've always loved to see Jake take an interest in music and, as he progressed on the fiddle, I'd invite him up onstage with me from time to time to help him build confidence and get used to performing in front of an audience.

One night, when I was about eighteen and he was ten, I took him with me to a gig at the Bolton Irish Centre. We went down a storm and everyone was impressed with the little guy on fiddle so, when the gig was over, I was over the moon when the organizer handed him £40 for his efforts. She handed me my money in an envelope too, and off we set home, chuffed to bits that Jake had been recognized for his talents. All the way back to Liverpool, I preached to him about the importance of keeping up his music.

'Imagine how long it would take you to earn that in another job,' I told him as I drove along the road. 'And there you are, less than half an hour on stage and you earned money doing something that you absolutely loved. How does that feel?'

'Amazing!' said Jake from the front seat, clutching his forty pounds with a grin on his face like a Cheshire cat. It was honestly like Christmas had come early to him – forty whole big pounds was a very big deal to such a little boy, and I was the proud and oh so smug big brother who had shown him the way.

We told Mum and Dad when we got home and I was praised for showing such a good example. They were so impressed and applauded us both for doing such a great job and me for nurturing Jake's talent and giving him the opportunity . . . but my smugness soon left me when I opened up my own envelope to find that the very kind lady who paid Jake for his short but sweet performance had actually taken the forty quid off me to give to him! I was fuming, but I couldn't make a fuss after accepting such adulation and, even though I did tell Jake, there was no way he was giving me that forty quid back! In fact, he enjoyed spending it even more after hearing that!

While Jake and I are both very musical, we are not very mechanical, unfortunately, so when we had a bit of an incident on the road one evening on our way to our aunty's house to pick up some ironing we had to call in some assistance. There we were, hurtling along the winding roads – I was probably driving too fast, as I admit to doing back then – when my Renault Kangoo van spun, I lost control and we almost crashed into a wall. We got out to check out the damage and, when we saw that one of the wheels needed changing, there was no way we were calling Dad, who would have taken the mickey out of us for not being able to change it ourselves. To shield our embarrassment, we ended up ringing my friend John, who came along and saved the day, but when we got home and Dad saw the spare wheel on the van we had to come clean. I must admit he was a lot more concerned about the near-miss we'd had with a wall than the flat tyre!

Those early days on the road with my little brother were great fun, and I worked hard to show him a good example, which I think has paid off a bit, as he is now doing so well for himself in the industry with his success in the Irish version of *Strictly Come Dancing*, which is called *Dancing with the Stars*, playing the title role of Aladdin at the SSE Arena and gigging his own music, which is more of a pop blend in style rather than the country flavour my work leans to. We live together now in Fermanagh and we're probably closer than ever, though neither of us is very domesticated! Well, Jake is probably a bit tidier than I am, if the truth be told, but I'm hardly ever there these days and, when I am, washing and ironing is not top of my list of favourite things to do, but we both manage somehow. Mum calls it a doss house, where all we do is sleep and eat, and I'd say she has a point! We spend our days off in summer on Lough Erne doing watersports, we go to the cinema together sometimes, and a real treat is to catch a live band, even if it's just one man on a guitar. It's one of our favourite ways to hang out and chill together.

Jake winds me up, as he's a real gym bunny, where I tend to need a bit more convincing. He always says I'm first into the steam room or the jacuzzi rather than working out! I am getting better at it, though . . .

I love to encourage my brother and sister in any way I can, and I feel that, as the eldest in the family, it's my duty to lead by example, so I've tried to share any contacts with Jake and made introductions for him to help him get his own career off the ground. He's super-talented and I'm so proud of him, and I love to see him get so passionate about what he does, as it really does take every ounce of blood, sweat and tears to make it in the music industry. He's a hard worker and puts all his energy into his career, which I really admire. I see a lot of it in myself too.

That strive, that ambition to succeed, most definitely comes from our father, Ian, who worked so hard all our lives, teaching us that, if we want something badly enough, we have to work our asses off to get it.

Dad works as a builder and he always inspired me in every way with his work ethic, plus, I owe him a lot for showing and guiding me on how to build a property portfolio. He was always juggling about ten things at once and is very good at multitasking, which I know is something most of us men are accused of not being very skilled at! He was always on the go when we were growing up, and he showed us how to invest in our passion. His passion was buying and renovating houses, something he still enjoys doing to this day. I think I take after him in many ways, as I too am always doing something and I find it hard to switch off. Even on my days off I'm never really off at all. My phone is constantly ringing and I'll pace the floors while taking calls – a sign, my mother always says, of me taking too much on, but she knows it's in my nature, and I definitely get it from my dad.

My mum, Noreen, is very much a people person, and that's probably where I take after her the most, as I've always been the same, happiest mingling and chatting to others. She has great empathy and loves people no matter who they are or where they come from, and she's taught me to always treat people the same. She is very patient and kind and I hope that has rubbed off on me when it comes to meeting people through my work in the music industry. I appreciate so much that people have often travelled to my gigs and I try and give everyone a bit of my time afterwards in a bid to show some appreciation, though sometimes I take it a bit too far and find it hard to disengage, ending up even more exhausted than I should be. I guess it's all about finding a happy medium, but I'm working on that!

Growing up, our grandparents were a huge part of our life and, for me, this was really the case once Jake and Kiara came along, as my mum was so busy with them and sometimes Nan and Grumps would take me off her hands so that she'd one less to worry about.

In 1999, when I was nine years old, just before the big Millennium celebrations came around, my grandmother Amana was planning one of her super parties, as she did every Christmas. There was great excitement and everyone – all the extended family – were invited. This was going to be a party like no other and Amana had spent weeks and weeks in the run-up to Christmas planning it for us all. We had just moved into a new house, so Mum offered to host a Millennium party for New Year, which added to the excitement, but one day in December, just a few days before Christmas, our landline rang and we got the most awful news.

'John has fallen down the stairs,' said Amana to my mum. 'He's on life support. It's not good.'

Grandad John was in his seventies and was of fine health, so this was a huge shock to us all, especially Amana, of course, who loved him so much, just as every one of his huge family did. My dear old grandad John had taught me my first tune on the accordion and now here he was, hanging on for his life at my family's most favourite time of the year. It just seemed so cruel to happen at Christmas, when we had a new house and there was so much to celebrate. I remember the confusion as a nine-year-old boy, torn between the excitement of Santa coming and my new bedroom and so much to explore in the neighbourhood, with the overhanging change of mood as everyone feared the worst for Grandad John, who lay in hospital between Christmas and New Year.

My beloved grandfather passed away just a few days before the Millennium, so he didn't get to see it through, as he'd so hoped to. His loss was a big shock to my dad, and I too was devastated. I'd never known life without my two sets of grandparents, who gave us so much of their time and attention, and it all just seemed wrong, like a mistake, that this had happened to us in the midst of such happiness. Mum tried to keep everything ticking along over the festivities for our sake, and she even went ahead with a much lower key Millennium gathering, really just as an excuse to have everyone together at such a tough time, which I think helped us all a lot, including Nana Amana, who stayed with us a bit after that at weekends, as she didn't like to be on her own all the time. That's the best thing about being part of such a big family. When times get rough, we all rally together and, even though she still loved her independence, Amana knew that there was always room at our house when she needed it.

We lost Amana nine years after Grandad John died, and

not having them certainly has left a big hole in my life, plus, I feel so bad for my dad now, not having either of his parents around. I am so close to my own parents, and I don't know what I'd do without them. Even though I don't see them as often as I'd like to any more, I always know that they are on the end of the phone, and there's nothing quite like getting home to Liverpool, where I'll just be Nathan again, like I never even left there in the first place.

Mum says the house is a lot quieter now, and she misses the door knocking and all the noise and commotion that comes with three kids in the house but, thankfully, we all have the happiest of memories to look back on and, when we do get together as a family, I know by the beaming smile on Mum's face that it's her favourite thing in the world.

I have so much to be grateful for, I really have, and I'll never forget it. I was encouraged every step of the way by my parents and both sets of grandparents, who all loved to hear me play music and applauded and cheered the loudest with every single achievement, even when I was only starting out, in my primary-school days.

By the time I was set to leave primary school, my piano and accordion skills were beginning to come along nicely. I had learned a lot from my early lessons with Kathleen and my many days at Comhaltas, but perhaps one of my most valuable assets was one that would be developed more wholly in the next leg of my education.

That asset was my singing voice, and I was about to get a taste of what it was like to sing around the world. A whole new opportunity was just around the corner.

4. All Together Now

The world-famous robed boys' choir of St Francis Xavier College in Woolton, Liverpool, was founded in 1994 by Keith Knowles, who was then Director of Music at the school, which I moved to when I was eleven years old. St Francis Xavier is an all-boys grammar school (co-educational in the sixth form), and the choir was very renowned by the time I joined there, and places in it very exclusive. Only eight to ten newcomers were selected out of around a hundred first-years who would audition each year. I was so thrilled to be selected as one of them not long after I started at the school.

Although there weren't any tears on my first day at St Francis Xavier, like there were on my first day at primary school, it was a very daunting experience to be moving from the small, cosy walls of Bishop Eton to the long corridors and numerous classrooms of grammar school, plus, I wouldn't be getting away with pulling any sickies here, as I didn't have Nan next door to come and bail me out when I fancied a change of scenery!

As well as being home to a *Guinness Book of Records* world-record-breaking choir that sang in every cathedral in England and Wales, St Francis's College also specialized in maths and computing, which were subjects I managed to keep on top of to the best of my ability. We wore a maroon blazer to school, and some of the famous names who attended included the BAFTA-winning scriptwriter Jimmy McGovern and several professional footballers, including Jon Flanagan

(Liverpool FC) and Tony Warner, as well as the Laurence Olivier Award-winning musical-theatre actor Michael Xavier.

My main interest wasn't maths or computing, though; it was of course the music room, and I'd be known to skip PE in favour of going there and playing some tunes, which was almost unheard of, being from a city that is immersed in blue and red and known for its love of football. I'm always asked by well-meaning football fans if I support Liverpool FC or Everton FC and, to be honest, it's just not my thing at all, but if push came to shove, I'd probably sway towards the reds. Despite my lack of interest in the holy national sport, in a big twist of irony it was a link to football that gave me one of my most memorable moments of my life when I performed with the school choir and made my first major television appearance.

The year was 2004, I was just thirteen years old and, by then, I had been promoted to Head Chorister of the choir. It was a role that I took very seriously – it was a massive honour to be selected out of so many talented singers to take it on.

The job of Head Chorister meant that I had to lead by example, both with the singing and for the overall reputation of the choir and, with three years of experience in the choir now under my belt, it was also my job to look out for the junior members and make sure they were all on their best behaviour. Not that I always led by example outside of school hours . . .

Like most boys and girls of our age, my friends and I were known to get up to all sorts of rascality in a harmless enough way and, for my thirteenth birthday party, six of my friends went bowling and one of my friends, Anthony, disappeared to the toilets, only to return with a condom pulled over his head. This amused us all no end, until Anthony couldn't get the condom off again and my dad had to intervene and cut it off, which he wasn't impressed by, though secretly I'd say he was laughing his head off behind it all!

Schoolboy antics aside and back to that big TV moment with the choir, it really was a great time to be involved in anything artistic in Liverpool, as it was announced in 2004 that the city was to be European Capital of Culture in 2008. The leader of Liverpool City Council at the time, Mike Storey, said it was like 'Liverpool winning the Champions League, Everton winning the double and the Beatles re-forming all on the same day – and Steven Spielberg coming to the city to make a Hollywood blockbuster about it.'

Our taste of fame with the choir was a bit more modest in stature than all of that, but an amazing experience nonetheless for twenty-four of us when Peter Hooton, the lead singer of the Merseyside band The Farm heard us singing one of his songs, 'All Together Now', at that year's Hillsborough Memorial Service at Anfield. Peter immediately contacted the school to invite us to accompany his band on a new recording of the song, which was about socialism, brotherhood and football and had been written by Hooton when he was in his twenties. Our new version would go on to be the anthem for the England football team in the Euro 2004 Finals which took place in Portugal in June and July that year. The song had previously been in the charts twice, with the original version peaking at number four in the UK charts and then becoming a hit for the second time when it was used by Everton in 1995, the year they won the FA Cup.

Our 2004 version was edited by DJ Spoony and recorded at Elevator Studios on Cheapside in Liverpool, a huge converted warehouse where artists such as Echo and The Bunnymen, Texas and The Kooks recorded.

It's hard to describe just how amazing the whole 'All

Together Now' experience was as the weeks passed by and the song became more and more popular. We were in all the newspapers, we were interviewed on the radio, and everyone, including the City Council, was immensely proud of us, describing us as 'wonderful ambassadors for the city'. We even received a gold disc for our part in the song, which shot into the charts the moment it was released.

Top of the Pops, the most iconic music-chart programme of its time, which was broadcast once a week for decades upon decades, was recorded at the BBC studios in the bright lights of London, and the episode we were on was presented by Fearne Cotton, so the excitement of the twenty-four boys who had been selected from the forty-two-strong school choir was electric.

After being presented with our gold disc at school by Demon Group Records, we set off for London to perform the song (you can still watch it on YouTube). It features a lot of close-ups of me, in my red-and-white robes for most of the song, before a change to the original lyrics where we all chanted 'All Together Now for England' and threw off our robes to reveal England football strips underneath. We then had to make our way to the front of the stage, where we gathered around Peter and sang those words to a huge, chanted finish. The audience clapped and screamed with pride.

Although not a huge football fan like most of the others, the rush of performing to the audience, the zooming in and out of the TV cameras, the heat of the blue-and-red lights, the mist from the dry ice that filled the studio and the beat of the music that pumped through me made my heart rush and, once again, I was reminded that this was what I wanted to do more than anything else in the whole world.

I couldn't believe it when I saw that the show we were on would also feature performances by Jessica Simpson singing

'With You', Peter Andre singing 'Insania' and my very first celebrity crush, Emma Bunton, who was now forging her own solo career after the Spice Girls. I don't think she noticed me, though . . .

Back at home, I secretly had my eye on a girl in our group of friends called Rebecca Benson, who I suppose was my first real-life teenage crush. Rebecca was tall, blonde, very attractive and the life and soul of the party, but there was one big problem – she was going out with one of my best friends, Anthony, and continued to do so for around six years, so all I could do was admire her from afar. We all kept in touch a lot by good old-fashioned telephone in those days and I recall running up a bill of £160 chatting to Rebecca, all in the spirit of friendship, of course, as she didn't see me as anything other than that and I'd never have tried to come between her and Anthony. I was just happy to be her friend and to spend time in her company, which I enjoyed doing in between school and choir life, which, in those early teenage years, took up a lot of my time.

Things showed no sign of settling down for the choir, and we were all still on a high from receiving our Gold Disc when we set off that August in 2004 on an American tour. Here, we got to visit New York, Washington and Boston, and being part of such an exclusive and successful school choir, not to mention all the travel and experiences it brought my way, really did improve my confidence onstage. I took on many solo parts in my role as Head Chorister, as well as having the comfort of performing with a large group of friends who knew how to have plenty of fun as well as put in the hours of practice it took to keep up the high standard of singing that was by now expected of us.

Being Head Chorister and singing on *Top of the Pops* gave me great confidence, so much so that I entered a singing competition called Teen Idol, where the top ten entrants, of which I was one, got to sing in the grand final at the Liverpool Philharmonic Hall. I chose the song 'When You Say Nothing at All' by Alison Krauss, which was made popular in the UK by Ronan Keating, and when I stepped out on to the huge stage in front of 1,600 people, it was a very different experience to singing with the choir. I was petrified! I didn't win, but the judges were very kind in their comments, complimented the tone of my voice and told me to keep on singing, as I had great potential. Overall, it was a challenge that stood me well, as it was my first time singing in front of so many people on my own.

Outside of the choir and any Teen Idol ambitions, my love of traditional Irish music, which continued out of school hours, also brought many opportunities for travel my way, and after years of touring the circuits as part of a competition called Fleadh Ceoil, a huge opportunity was about to come my way across the Irish Sea.

5. Ceoil, Craic and Céilí Bands

For anyone who hasn't been to a fleadh (pronounced *flaa*) in Ireland, it's a true experience like no other for anyone who loves Irish traditional music and a good old party and, for me and the rest of my family, it has been an annual event since I was about ten years old.

The annual All Ireland Fleadh is a celebration of Irish music and culture in a huge carnival-style atmosphere with dancing on the streets morning, noon and night; people of all ages play music outside shops, in bars and in community halls and there is a host of pageants, marching bands, drama performances and exhibitions. It's attended by tens of thousands of people from all over the world, including me, my mum and dad, my sister and brother and, of course, Nan and Grumps.

The big event is held each year in a different town which could be anywhere in Ireland and, through attending the Fleadh, we got to experience many wonderful places across the length and breadth of Ireland, such as the market town of Listowel in County Kerry, the island town of Ennis in County Clare, and the colourful streets of Clonmel in County Tipperary. No matter where the Fleadh was held, it was always great fun, and in every place we visited we met up with old and new friends, heard the best of new music and made lots of new memories. We'd pack up the car and sail across on the ferry in late August every year, then find our accommodation, which was normally a bed and breakfast or a small hotel near the main events, and we'd make a holiday of it while we lapped up the atmosphere and took in the music and the craic.

One of my favourite memories of attending the All Ireland Fleadh was in the year 2000, when it came to Enniscorthy, a very historic town in County Wexford on the east coast of Ireland which was described by James Joyce in *Ulysses* as the 'finest place in the world'. We were booked in to stay in a caravan overlooking nearby Curracloe Beach, famous for being one of the locations of the 1998 American epic war film *Saving Private Ryan* starring Tom Hanks. As a ten-year-old boy who had rarely stayed in a caravan before, I was super-excited at the adventure that lay ahead. I had travelled across from Liverpool on this occasion with Mum and Dad, Jake, Kiara and the double buggy that came everywhere with us, and we rang ahead to Nan and Grumps, who had already arrived at the caravan.

'It's like a tin shed with mouldy windows,' Grumps said, touching the mould with his finger in horror. Nan, who stood beside him, seemed equally dismayed as she looked around her.

'It's so old!' said Nan. 'It's about thirty *years* old. We can't stay here. It's freezing!'

We arrived at the caravan, and I loved it! I couldn't believe that it had a living room, a kitchen, a toilet and, best of all – bunkbeds! I gushed to them how amazing the caravan was and how much I totally loved it. As townies brought up in a big city like Liverpool, staying in that caravan was a big adventure for us, and I remember Jake looking out of the window in awe at the sheep and cows in the field right beside us.

That night, the heavens burst open with a storm complete with thunder and lightning, and Nan and Grumps packed up to go and find a hotel. The rest of us stayed on, and I enjoyed every moment of it, though I do admit to getting the best of both worlds by staying at the hotel with Nan and Grumps the odd night too!

The great thing about the Fleadh moving to different towns each year was that my family got to make a holiday of it, sightseeing (for some reason, the weather always seemed to be better when I was younger, despite that storm), while I prepared to take part in the more serious side of things – the competition. The main competitions are a major part of the Fleadh and seek out the finest in a wide range of talent. Only the best get the chance to compete, and I was lucky enough to qualify from the British heats on many occasions in categories such as piano, solo accordion, lilting, solo singing, céilí bands and other duets and trios. Adjudicators who specialize in each section watch competitors perform in front of an audience and decide who deserves the much-coveted All Ireland title. It was always my dream to go back to Liverpool with a title under my belt, because to win an All Ireland medal was the highest honour in the traditional-music world. From the age of ten, I made it so close, year in, year out, but I just couldn't seem to break through to get the main prize. The competition was fierce, and I remember some of the young musicians who were just unbeatable and who would win every year, it seemed, but I kept on trying, hoping that my time would come.

Back at home in Liverpool, I played accordion with the under-twelve céilí band, which was a great training ground for each year's big competition across the Irish Sea. We played in regional competitions, which was great for my confidence, and we'd practise every Monday night at St Michael's Irish Centre, which I really enjoyed. Then, when I was about thirteen or fourteen, I was asked on occasion to step in with the senior céilí band – quite an honour for someone so young. Sean McNamara (or Sean Mac, as he was fondly known) was the band leader, and he used to pick me up every week when I was needed, and off we'd go to various functions such as social events and Irish weddings across the north-west of England. Sean was a fine fiddle player and a great mentor to me, not to mention the added bonus that I'd get paid for such events – the grand sum of £50 for just an hour or so of playing music. Considering I was working on a paper round each morning back then that earned me £25 for five mornings' work, I started to realize that doing something I loved the most in the world – playing music – could also have very nice financial rewards when you got to a certain level.

I was thrilled and honoured to be acknowledged for my music, particularly in my role as Head Chorister with the school choir when, in April 2003, I was shortlisted as a Merseyside and Cheshire Young Achiever at a gala dinner and awards ceremony in Liverpool Town Hall organized by the NCH (National Childrens' Home, now Action for Children). The event aimed to publicly recognize some of the area's young people in categories such as arts, sports, unsung heroes and learning, and the winner of the sports award that night was none other than England international and then Evertonian Wayne Rooney, who had recently celebrated his eighteenth birthday. Even though I can't claim to be a football fan, being included in a list of honours along with Wayne was an achievement for me in itself – you can imagine the delight on Grumps' face when he realized the fine company we would be mixing in that night, even though Wayne was a blue and he was a red!

My time as a young teenager was certainly well packed: school during the day, my commitments to the choir, then practice every Monday with the céilí band, not to mention my lessons in singing and piano. I learned so much from playing in the senior céilí band at St Francis Xavier, and I was way younger than anyone else in the band so I'd take in as much as I could by watching and listening to the older musicians, determined to use all the experience I could muster to get to Ireland and win that big title once and for all.

Each year, the week before the All Ireland Fleadh was spent at a specialist Irish traditional music 'school' called Scoil Éigse which ran during the day from Monday to Friday, and it was a great benefit to us competitors, who were given the opportunity to learn from the finest in the business. We'd work really hard during the day, and at night we'd be allowed to go out to play music in the nearby pubs in *seisuns*, which again would leave me in awe as I watched and listened and learned from the very best musicians that Ireland had to offer. It's funny how, at the age of fourteen or fifteen and even younger, it was perfectly fine to be in the pub at night at the Fleadh because you were playing music when, the rest of the year, it would probably be frowned upon. The Fleadh was very much a family affair and it was part of the experience to see young teenagers and children joining in with their instruments at every given opportunity. The rush we would feel would be totally electric, and I'd look forward to going there year after year after year, even if I still hadn't won, after coming so close on every occasion.

In late August 2005 my family made our usual trip to the Fleadh, this time to the cathedral town of Letterkenny in County Donegal, where I was set to compete in the singing, piano and lilting (a form of traditional singing) finals, having made it through once again from the British heats, which I have to admit was already a great honour. To even get that far each year, you'd have to come top in the north-west regional heat, and then compete against the southern England finalists to eventually come up against the All Britain competitors, who would also include a lot of mighty fine talented Scottish singers and musicians. So the competition even to get to the All Ireland finals was very tough, and here I was again, on the way to Letterkenny to give it another shot.

I attended the Scoil Éigse as usual the week before, where I absorbed as much as I could possibly take in from those teaching us in each day's masterclasses. I had two songs to learn for the competition final – an Irish song called *Erin Grá Mo Chroí* ('Ireland, Love of My Heart') and 'The Bodhrán Song', which was about the life of a goat who was about to become the skin of a bodhrán! I practised those songs everywhere I went, listening to as many different versions and recordings as I could get my hands – or should I say my ears? – on, and I was so determined to get the pronunciation of Gaelic words right, never mind the melodies, so I sang and sang them again and again, pacing the corridors and going over them in my head on the morning of the competition.

When it came to my turn I took to the stage with my heart thumping, hoping at last to win that big prize of first place. There were twelve or so competitors in my heat and I took a deep breath, catching sight of Nan in the audience. She always gave me a sign that she is there – she'd put her hand through her hair so that I'd notice her. This was a vote of confidence, as it meant I could find my family in the audience and I didn't feel so alone up there on that lonely stage with all at stake when I wanted to win so badly.

I took another breath and then I began, and once I got into the song the nerves left me, as they usually did, and I sang both *Erin Grá Mo Chroí* and 'The Bodhrán Song' as best I could. I waited for my applause and took my seat back in the audience. The tension mounted as the adjudicators made their notes, then silently left us to hold our breath until they returned with their decision.

They called out the winner of third place. It wasn't me.

I gulped and closed my eyes.

Then the name of the winner in second place. Again, it wasn't me.

I closed my eyes and hoped for the best. Not coming second or third could mean I hadn't been placed at all, or, on the other hand, it could mean that I'd done it at last. Could this be it? Could this be the year it would finally be me?

'The winner . . .' said the adjudicator '. . . the winner of the solo singing category . . . we have to give it to Nathan Carter of Liverpool.'

My heart soared. I'd done it! After years of competing in various elements of the famous All Ireland Fleadh I was finally an All Ireland champion for singing! I couldn't stop smiling as my family grinned from ear to ear and hugged me tight in celebration.

In the traditional-music world, I'd gone as far as I could in terms of acknowledgement for my talents, and the rush I felt inside at hitting that milestone made me even more determined that this was what I wanted to do for the rest of my life.

It was a huge honour for me to go back to Liverpool with that medal. I took great pleasure in sharing the success with the Comhaltas, with the céilí band and all who had helped me to get this far.

The sense of achievement proved to me that, when you put in the work for something you want so badly, anything is possible. I wanted to play music as a career. I wanted to be a singer. I just had to figure out how it was all going to work out – but one person very close to me had a good idea as to how it was all going to pan out, as she believed in me every step of the way.

That person was someone most of you know already. That person was my nan.

6. Me and My Nan

Throughout the 1990s and right up until about six years ago, Nan ran a guesthouse called The Real McCoy in Liverpool. I spent many days of my childhood there, meeting people from all walks of life who came to stay.

The Real McCoy was a cosy piece of heaven housed in a five-bedroom semi about four miles out of the city centre, near where the TV soap operas *Brookside* and *Hollyoaks* were made. The house was always packed with guests involved in the shows or with Irish people who were across for music or a weekend break. Hope Park University was also on the doorstep, which meant teachers and lecturers would be regular visitors, and there would also be guests from America who were over for events, so Nan had a great market right outside her door.

The house wasn't decorated in any fancy way but, for some reason, Nan did have a fondness for cherub figurines, and they were everywhere – on the tables, as lamp bases, on the mantelpiece – any sort of ornament, if it was available as a cherub, Nan had it! She also took great pride in the internal glass panel doors which were a feature in the house. Sadly, they were taken out when new fire regulations came in, and she had to get rid of her fancy handles, much to her despair.

Nan's house was comfy and homely and she made a hearty breakfast which everyone who stayed there would comment on fondly, plus, Grumps would be up every morning before the guests got out of bed, playing his Irish or country music (maybe to the guests' annoyance!), and he loved to chat to everyone, finding out all the gossip, like where they had been the night before and any news they might have to share with him. People got to know and love them both, which added to the whole experience, as did the outside toilet that Grumps insisted on keeping, even when my dad renovated the place and put on an extension. Grumps always had an outside toilet when he was growing up and he felt it added character to the place, plus, he liked to escape out there for the peace, even though it was freezing cold!

At Christmas time The Real McCoy was like the League of Nations. We never knew who would be round Nan's table; sometimes there could be twenty people staying there. As one of ten children, Nan loved to entertain and to cook, and there was always food on the go and a real family atmosphere. Some of the regular guests even had their own key to the house and could come and go as they pleased.

People came from far and wide to avail themselves of her renowned hospitality and everyone would be given a welcome drink on arrival to her house, while visitors used to bring her chocolates and flowers to say thank you for her kindness.

As well as looking after people in her busy bed and breakfast, Nan also looked after people in the wider community through her other role as manager of the local social club for fourteen years.

The social club, or the Parish Centre, as it was also known, was a big Georgian house with a function room that, as I've said, seemed massive to me at the time. Looking back, it probably wasn't as big as I imagined it. There was a bar and a kitchen with cellars underneath where all the barrels were kept; this is where Grumps would do the stocktaking. I used to help out by rolling the barrels down to the cellar, and

Grumps would tell me stories about the ghosts who lived there, which I loved to hear.

To me, the Parish Centre was the most exciting place in the world. There was always something happening, from weddings to christenings, and Nan was always at the heart of it, running the bar, overseeing the catering and taking bookings for Irish dancing classes, line dancing classes and other cultural and arts activities. The place was full of characters from all walks of life and the smell of smoke would knock you sideways, though you sometimes wouldn't notice it until the next day, when there'd be a stench off your clothes.

I loved listening to characters like Danny Dunne who played 'Whiskey in the Jar' and 'Tell Me Ma' on the guitar, and I'd join in, stopping only to munch on a bag of bacon fries or scampi fries, which I'd help myself to from behind the bar.

There was always a hive of music in the Parish Centre, and guests like The Hilton Showband, who were friends of Nan's parents back in Newry, would pop across for a gig and stay the weekend at The Real McCoy.

Being of a similar nature to Nan and Grumps, I loved to be around the bed and breakfast as well as the Parish Centre, and I'd often be found in either place with Nan, chipping in with a bit of help around the kitchen or, more like it, talking to all the people who would come and go every day or trying my best to entertain them with my songs and accordion!

Aside from our love of talking and socializing, the biggest thing my nan and I have always had in common is of course our great lifelong love of music. She loved to see me being invited up on stage at the social centre to play accordion with the guest musicians, and once I even got to play on a piano that had been donated by Chris de Burgh. I played 'Galway Girl', and I could barely even reach the keys!

I was in adult company a lot as a child, but I don't think it ever did me any harm; in fact, it helped my confidence and communication skills a lot, as I was always encouraged to take part in conversation and, with music, I always had something to talk about.

I always said my nan could sell snow to Eskimos and, when I started to gig at local functions such as weddings and events in my early teens, she was my biggest promoter. She was a powerhouse back then, working all day at the Parish Centre while managing the bed and breakfast, sometimes not making it home until about 3 a.m., then she'd be up again at six making breakfast for all her visitors. She was a real night owl and, even now, at the grand age of seventy-eight, she just gets up and gets on with it, no matter how little sleep she's had the night before.

Nan never failed to miss an opportunity to tell anyone she met that I could sing and play music, sometimes much to my embarrassment. One St Patrick's Day when I was only about ten years old, we were at St Laurence's Irish Community Centre in Liverpool when one of those opportunities arose.

Singing on stage was a Manchester man of Armagh descent called Nicky James who would later become very influential in my early career, but Nicky has a funny memory of that particular day when Nan brought me in to the gig.

'For God's sake, if that woman asks you to take that boy up on stage, tell her no,' said the former County Cavan footballer Phil Farley, who was running the place.

But Nan didn't *ask* Nicky if I could go on stage, she *told* him so, and before long I was up there, playing a few tunes on the accordion, and the audience (and Nicky) loved it. That was the type of her and still is. She is full of determination and won't ever let anyone stop her in her tracks when she has something on her mind to do with my music.

Another one of my favourite places to go with Nan was to the wholesalers when she needed to stock up for the B&B and the social centre. She drove a little two-door Honda Civic and she'd ask if I wanted to bring a friend to keep me company, which I always did, and we used to climb into the back of the car, where the seats would be down, and because Nan drove like Michael Schumacher, when she'd slam on the brakes it would make us roll around in the back, which we thought was the best fun ever. Not safe at all, of course, but we absolutely loved it. When we'd get to the wholesalers my friend and I would be too young to get in, as it was only for adults, but Nan would hide us in the trolley which of course led to even more giggling and laughing along the way.

Nan was always spoiling me. She even bought me my first mobile phone as a birthday present, when I was about thirteen years old. It was the best thing ever – I was linked up to the 121 Network and I thought I was great, texting my friends and playing Snake at every opportunity I could get around school and my music.

Nan has always had a taste for the finer things in life, and she loves spending money. She loves *making* money, but she loves *spending* it just the same, much to Grumps' bemusement, and one job she fell into allowed her to sample the high life in a way she never had before.

Through her many different roles in the community, Nan got to know a man called Norman Gard who was the liaison officer for Liverpool Football Club. Part of Norman's job was to do airport pick-ups and sort out travel for players, and sometimes he'd ask Nan to help out and lend her his grand big Mercedes Benz for a couple of days. Nan would cruise around in Norman's car thinking she was a multimillionaire, down to London and back again with some of football's biggest names as her passengers, and she came to know the very famous Liverpool FC manager Gerard Houllier very well. She loved to boast about this, so it was quite an embarrassment to her when she was sent to pick him up one day not in the big fancy Merc, which was unavailable, but in her own trusty two-door Honda Civic. Talk about being brought back down to earth with a bump! She wasn't impressed one bit, and I'm sure Gerard was a bit confused too, and from that day on she always dreamed of owning her very own Mercedes Benz.

When Nan eventually gave up the Parish Centre after those fourteen years, she at last had some free time on her hands, and she didn't know what to do with it. By this time, I was becoming busier in the evenings, as gigs began to trickle in at different Irish centres across the north-west of England for weddings, christenings, birthday parties, and so on, but of course I was too young to drive, so a new job for Nan was created. She was never asked to drive me to gigs, she just wanted to help, and she slotted into the role perfectly, as once again she was in her glory, always on the move and getting out and about to meet new people.

During our travels to my gigs Nan and I bonded more and more, and I could always go to her if I was ever worried about anything. My cousins and my siblings joke that I'm the golden child in her eyes, as we were always together and there are a lot more photos of me in her house than there are of any of the others, but I always claimed that it's because I was the first grandchild, plus, I was also an only child for six years (though, secretly, I know that we do have a very special relationship). At times when I'd feel a bit jaded about going to lessons or maybe was tired and not overly enthused about heading out to gigs, Nan was always there at my back, encouraging me and urging me not to give it up and, boy, am I glad she stuck by me and made sure I kept it going!

We had no satnav in those early days, of course, so we'd often get lost trying to find venues, and we still had that secret code from before where she'd pretend to fix her hair when I was on stage so that I could see she was there when I was singing. Nan loved being on the road, she loved meeting people, so her new role really suited her and she was always up for the challenge.

Even now, Nan is a big part of the team when we are on the road. She is the one in charge of all the merchandise, and she has been known to order everything from Nathan Carter calendars to mugs to CDs and even pillowcases – I often wonder what on earth she will come up with next! Even her accordion handbag is legendary and is now a familiar sight on the stall which she sets up on every night of every tour, proudly chatting to fans of all ages from all parts of the country.

We've spent so much time together since I was a baby, and there's no doubt about it, I have a special bond with her that could never be broken. She still looks out for me, even though I'm grown up now, and I know I can still tell her anything if I'm worried or if I just need a friendly ear. I'm so proud to be living in the country she came from and carrying on her family tradition and love of Irish and country music, and I know that I make her proud every day and she makes me proud too, with her enthusiasm, her drive and her infectious personality. I often think of her mother, my great Nana Winifred from County Down, who I never got to meet. I hope that we are all making her proud too as she watches over us.

Nan loves the Phil Coulter song 'The Town I Loved So Well', so I dedicate it to her at every opportunity, which I suppose is like my own secret code back to her after all these years to tell her how much I still appreciate her support.

In fact, I try to show her my appreciation in any way I possibly can, so you can imagine the delight on her face when, just a couple of years ago, I decided to try and reward her for all the years she has invested in me and my career while juggling her own commitments as a mother, aunt, grandmother and so much more. I really wanted to give her something to say a big thank you, so I bought her something special for her seventy-sixth birthday present. With some help from my dad, we got it from Manchester to Liverpool safely, hid it in the garage at her home in Liverpool and waited for her to come home.

The present I chose for her had had one lady owner, was a few years old, had low mileage and two doors, just like her famous old Honda Civic back in the day, but it was a lot sportier than the Civic and a bit more exciting!

As Mum, Dad, Grumps and my sister Kiara led her into the garage, I watched from Ireland on Facetime and, when she was handed the keys, there wasn't a dry eye. As soon as she spotted her present, she couldn't stop crying, and everyone joined in.

Nan cruises about now, feeling just like the millionaire she did when she used to drive those footballers around, but now it's in her very own sporty little Mercedes Benz, and it does my heart good to see the smile on her face. It's the least I could do for her for all her continued support down the years.

To me, and to so many who know her, Nan is a one-off – a positive ball of energy. My mum reckons she was born with wheels on her feet, always ready for the next trip, no matter where it might be to. She is so young at heart, so full of spirit, and I've never met anyone like her and probably never will. She's terrible with money – awful, really – but, thankfully, Grumps keeps her right and, despite it, she is the best salesperson you will ever find.

Most of all, though, she's my biggest cheerleader and one of my very best friends, and no, she hasn't slowed down, and of course now she has her own Merc to drive around in, she still races about like Schumacher and slams on the brakes with only seconds' notice.

I must ask her someday if she fancies a spin to the wholesalers in the Merc, for old times' sake. At least I'd be allowed in this time and wouldn't have to hide in the trolley!

7. Sweet Sixteen

I was sixteen years old when I next met Nicky James, the Manchester singer with Armagh roots who I'd first come across as a ten-year-old at St Laurence's Irish Community Centre who Nan 'told' and didn't ask when it came to me joining him for a tune.

Nicky was a regular performer at the Liffey Bar on Renshaw Street in Liverpool, an Irish bar which had Sunday afternoon and evening gigs, so when some of his cousins were staying at the B&B for the Grand National, Nan suggested I go with them to hear Nicky sing and to see if he'd be interested in hearing how I'd progressed over the years.

I walked into the Liffey Bar that afternoon and the atmosphere hit me in the face. My jaw dropped open in awe. People were jumping around, singing and dancing, and the place was bouncing as Nicky belted out song after song after song. I couldn't believe how such a party was going on, here in this little pub, where this man had the audience eating out of his hands, and I imagined myself up there doing what he does and having such a good time with it all.

'What songs do you have?' he asked me later, and I gave him a home recording of a few folk songs I'd been doing the rounds with up until then.

Nicky says that when he heard my version of 'The Boys from Barr na Sràide' from that home recording he knew I had something special in my voice, and he agreed to help me.

Before long, he was regularly giving me gigs to help me try and get some experience of the pub scene, which I found to be a far cry from the smaller, cosier Irish ex-pat crowds I'd been playing to up until then. My first night in the Liffey Bar was the nine o'clock slot on a Sunday evening, and when I turned up there were just a few, quite drunk, stragglers left over from the earlier music sessions, so I found myself playing to about ten people – and that was including the bar staff and my dad, who had driven me there and helped me set up!

It was a humbling experience and a learning curve for me and, every day, I'd ring Nicky for advice. Sometimes in life, I believe, you meet people who mentor you and inspire you, not for any particular personal gain but just because perhaps they see something in you that they may believe in, or perhaps that they recognize in themselves, and that's how I felt when I met Nicky.

I found myself travelling as far as Halifax, Leeds and Manchester for pub gigs, and my confidence was slowly building, plus, I got to know which songs worked and which didn't.

'You need to make a proper CD,' said Nicky. 'We need a calling card to send out to venues and promoters if you want to take this seriously.'

And so we did just that. Watching and learning from Nicky made me want this more than ever, and soon we found ourselves in Redcar Studios under the guidance of Nicky's friend John Taylor, where we laid down twelve tracks of folk songs, including the ballads 'Carrickfergus', 'Isle of Innisfree', 'Working Man' and 'After All These Years'.

As I stood there in the studio for the first time on my own, without the comfort of the choir to sing along with me, I felt nervous, anxious and a bit afraid, plus, when they played back the tracks, initially I didn't really like the sound of my own voice. It was a bit like hearing yourself speak on a recording – it just didn't sound like me, and I was singing in a very different style by now, having left all the pronounced vowels and breathing techniques of the choir-boy training behind. But John Taylor and Nicky James were out to bring out the best in me and, as a first recording, they did just that, with high-quality recording equipment and attention to detail.

'He's the most complete singer ever to have recorded in my studio,' John Taylor said to Nicky at the time. 'Sometimes an artist can sound different when they get to the studio, but his sound is instantly brilliant. He just has it.'

Nicky also arranged for a photoshoot to go with the CD, which was to be named *Starting Out*, and I posed in a black suit for pictures on Rose Lane, thinking I was nice at the time, though I cringe when I look back on it now. I was only sixteen, though, and let's face it, most of us hate looking back at our style in our awkward teenage years, so maybe I shouldn't beat myself up too much about it.

Before the CD was ever pressed or printed Nan was working her magic once again and, when a Longford showband singer called Dermot Hegarty came to stay at her B&B she saw another opportunity. Dermot had heard of me (but then again, everyone who knew Nan had heard of me!) and he persuaded Gerry Flynn of Enjoy Travel, who arranged music holidays with special guests, to give me a slot on a forthcoming cruise that September for free.

This was a huge boost of confidence for me and it was a real coup to get a slot on the cruise, even though it was only a one-off and for half an hour in total.

There were only two problems with the whole possibility – one, that it clashed with back-to-school dates and two, I didn't have my CD ready yet.

'You can't go on the cruise without a CD,' Nan told me, wearing her permanent businesswoman thinking hat. 'When can the copies of your CD be ready?'

Not on time, it turned out, but that wasn't going to stop Nan, no way. She got on the phone and rang around every CD-printing firm she could find, eventually finding one in London that could print five hundred CDs in a two-day turnaround – but London was a four-hour drive away and I wasn't old enough to drive yet.

'I'll drive to London tonight to deliver the master copy,' Nan said, much to my parents' bewilderment. They hadn't fully decided if I could go on the cruise because of school commitments, as I was all set to do my A levels, and Mum had my new uniform bought and ready for my first day back.

Before anyone could discuss or question any further, Nan and I set off that night from Liverpool to deliver the songs to London with the address of the man, who had told us to post it through his letterbox. It was 3 a.m. when we made it to his house – my mum and dad thought we were crazy to be doing such a thing – but Nan had a vision in her head and nothing was going to stop her.

We posted it through the letterbox as instructed and set off on the journey back home again, making it back to Liverpool at around 7 a.m., absolutely exhausted but very pleased that our mission had been accomplished. Nan had it all figured out. Forty-eight hours would allow us just enough time to get on the cruise. Now all we had to do was convince my parents to let me go and pack my bag.

Could it really be so simple? Not quite, it turned out, because yes, we had delivered the master copy to London, yes, we had posted through a letterbox, but unfortunately, it was the wrong letterbox in the wrong apartment block and the man didn't get it!

Not to be beaten, Nan was on the ball first thing that morning again. She directed the man in London to the mistaken address and, lo and behold, we had the copies of the

CD in our hands within forty-eight hours, as promised. All we had to do now was convince my parents to let me miss a week of school at the beginning of such an important term.

'What about his A levels?' Mum asked. 'He can't be missing ten days at the start of term.'

I looked at my school uniform, knowing it would still be there when I got back. It was only ten days – would I really miss that much?

'That boy has all the A levels he needs in his voice, believe me,' said Nan. 'Plus, I've paid for a cabin already, so we may as well take it.'

'You've already got us a cabin?' I asked Nan. Grumps looked as shocked as I was. I didn't know she was so on the ball.

'Yes, we're in . . . look, I couldn't get anything other than the presidential suite so I've booked us in there. It's kind of like the penthouse in a hotel, I suppose. I'm sure it's lovely.'

Grumps looked like he was going to faint with shock. Mum and Dad spoke up.

'Well, if that's the case, you'd better get going, then,' Mum said.

At last! Good old Nan! I'd finally been given the green light by my parents and, before long, we were packing to go on the Mediterranean cruise – me, Nan, Grumps and our hot-off-the-press five hundred *Starting Out* CDs! School was going to have to wait for another ten days.

For six whole hours the following day we travelled to Southampton by coach, where we were to meet the *Pacific Princess* cruise ship, and for six whole hours poor Grumps sat in shock as he let the news sink in that the only room left by the time Nan got the go-ahead and booked our accommodation was none other than the presidential suite, which cost a whopping four grand – twice as much as a regular room – on *his* Mastercard! He absolutely lost it, but that was typical of Nan. She was forever buying things or booking things on a whim, and there was no way she was going to let cost get in the way of her grandson having the opportunity to perform alongside some of Irish country's big names. Grumps jokes to this day that he is still paying off the interest on that trip! His Mastercard got a real battering, but he also agrees, of course, that it was worth every penny, as it was another step towards the future we had all dreamed of – a future of me living my dream as a full-time entertainer.

As we queued up to go on the ship, the holiday atmosphere had well and truly begun, and even Grumps couldn't help but smile and sing along to the live music that entertained guests as they waited to board. The *Pacific Princess* only held around six hundred people, but it is one of the most famous cruise ships of modern times, as it was the original vessel that featured in the worldwide romantic comedy TV series *The Love Boat*. To me, it was paradise on water. I was totally in awe of all that was going on around me. I'd never experienced anything like this before. The country singer Sharon Turley led the sailing-away party as guests danced and sang their way through Security, everyone starting off as they would continue for ten whole days, singing and dancing along to the finest of country music, and there was me, wondering how on earth I was going to live up to their expectations.

Back in the presidential suite, with its huge dining room, living room, grand mirrors and fancy pictures on the walls, I really did feel like the president. It was even more exciting when I was meant to be in school. Life on board the *Pacific Princess* was of course way out of our normal holiday budget and a world away from the poky caravans we had stayed in back on our holidays in Ireland, and I couldn't help but chuckle as I remembered the rusty caravan by the beach which was so much fun at the time. The ship, to me, was breathtaking, and I was filled with a rush of adrenaline, hearing the music continue as I dressed for dinner in my borrowed tux, which was far too big for me, all set to tuck into the fancy dinner that we were to be treated to each evening.

The food on the ship was another story in itself. I think it was the first time I'd ever had a proper sit-down four-course meal and I never tasted food so fine in my whole life. I even treated myself to two desserts, something I could never get away with doing now, or I'd pile on weight, but as a growing teenager I'd a huge appetite, and this to me was heaven.

The whole experience just kept getting better, and I couldn't believe my eyes when one of the guests at our table was none other than Irish country legend Johnny McEvoy – one of the many singers I'd grown up listening to under Nan and Grumps' influence. Johnny's hits included 'Nora' and 'Mursheen Durkin'. He was one of my idols, to say the least, as I'd watched an old VHS of his RTÉ show on repeat in wonder at his songwriting ability and his distinctive voice, so to be able to sit at the same table, eat with him and have a conversation with him was a real treat.

'What's your big dream?' he asked me, and it didn't take me long to reply.

'I want to have my own live band and tour the circuit,' I told him, having listened to his tales of playing in some of the most iconic venues, including many I knew of in Liverpool.

'I don't think you should get a band,' he told me, in so many words.

'Why not?' I asked him, my eyes wide in anticipation.

'It's a lot of hard work,' he explained to me. 'Politics get in the way, ego gets involved and it takes a lot of commitment to keep it going.'

'Oh . . . I see,' I replied, somewhat disheartened.

It wasn't the answer I was expecting, but wise words none-theless from such an icon who I admired and respected, and I now know exactly what he meant back then when he advised me about the challenges of running a band. It can be a bit like a family, or even a marriage of sorts. It takes an obscene amount of effort to make it work, it doesn't always go the way you want it to when personalities and real life get in the way, but, as I sat on that cruise ship waiting on my turn to perform, I had a fire in my belly that just wasn't going to go out. If anything, rather than putting me off, Johnny's advice made me even more determined to make it work and to find a band like I had dreamed of.

The second day of the cruise took us to the famous Bay of Biscay, which lies along the northern coast of Spain. The water there was seriously rough, and I remember there were céilí dancers who were trying to do the 'Siege of Ennis', but when they danced to the right the ship went left, and when they danced to the left the ship went right, and they all just stopped and laughed their heads off, as there was no way they were going to be able to compete with the elements at sea!

As we sailed around the Med over the next few days we sang along to various singing stars, we laughed until we cried at Donegal comedian Conal Gallen and, when it came to my turn to sing, halfway through the ten-day cruise, I'd got to know many of the singers and musicians, as well as the guests who were there to enjoy the music, and I was ready for my first big showcase away from my beloved Liverpool and its surrounding towns.

I took to the stage on the cruise ship in my dicky bow and oversized tux, all ready for my half-hour slot. My voice quivered a little to begin with, but I soon settled in and sang a selection of songs off the CD I'd recently recorded, with Liz

Gordon backing me on piano and Cliff Austin on bass. I was singing with live musicians. I was performing to a new audience who had no idea who I was and, best of all, they were all listening and singing along. I was in my glory.

As I gave them songs that were now so familiar to me, including the very first song I ever learned from my Grandad Carter, 'Danny Boy', Nan went round the tables, selling the CDs we'd travelled so far to get printed at the last minute, and she sold loads of them as the music-loving audience clapped and gave positive feedback to my cruise-ship debut. I was chuffed to bits and on a real high from the response from the audience, and even more so when, to my great surprise and delight, I was offered future gigs on other music-holiday packages by the organizers, Enjoy Travel.

'You want me back?' I said to them.

'We'd like to have you, for sure.'

I couldn't believe my ears. I'd performed alongside bands such as The Bachelors, who were really big in the sixties, I was in the company of seasoned performers such as Conal Gallen, legends of country music like Johnny McEvoy, and they thought I was good enough to come back and do it all over again!

I was thrilled, and so was Nan. Even Grumps was smiling from ear to ear with pride, despite his Mastercard and the damage it took to get us there.

'I'd really love to,' I told the organizers.

'Yes, he'd really love to,' echoed Nan, still buzzing from the CD sales she'd made over the past few days and the possibility of an even bigger audience next time.

If I'd ever needed a sign that this was all meant to be, then I had it. Everything seemed to be falling into place – meeting Nicky when I did and all the gigs he gave me, recording the CD under his guidance, being offered the cruise-ship slot through Dermot Hegarty, getting the CD printed on time against the odds in London, and now, here I was with more gigs of this level within arm's reach. It looked like it was all going to plan.

There was only one thing in my way, however, and it was quite a big thing. My brand-new school uniform was hanging waiting in my bedroom, and whether I would return to complete my A levels along with my peers at St Francis Xavier in Liverpool was still up in the air.

Would I go back to school and finish what I'd started by doing my A levels, or would I give this all a real push and see where it would take me?

A major, life-changing decision was coming my way.

8. Labour Days

We arrived back in Liverpool on a real high after the cruise and the thought of going back to school filled me with dread, but I put on my school uniform and gave it a go, just to be totally sure I was on the right track. A few days in, however, I knew my heart wasn't in school at all any more so I arranged a meeting for my parents and me to talk to the headmaster, Mr Rippon, to discuss my future.

To my genuine surprise, Mr Rippon said he wasn't shocked at all by my decision. My track record with the choir and all its success, plus my Fleadh win and my ongoing musicality around the social-club scene had given him an understanding that it was genuinely what I wanted to do, and he wished me well.

He also told me that, if it didn't work out, the door would always be open for me to come back, which we were all delighted with.

I had five gigs lined up in my first month off school, and Dad claimed he needed a bit of help on an extension he was doing, but looking back, I think he was trying to teach me the value of money and the difference between doing a hard week's work outdoors and turning up to play a gig in a pub.

Having done my sums, I knew that this extra money – a whole £125 a week – could come in handy, as I really needed to start saving if I wanted to get my own sound equipment and eventually a van on the road. I couldn't depend on Nan to drive me round for ever, no matter how much she enjoyed it, so off I set to my job on the building site. To say it was a shock to the system is an understatement!

My alarm went off every morning at seven o'clock and I would totally dread the sound of it each day. I could still tell you the pitch and every note of it as I woke up on those dark winter mornings and set out with Dad in the van in all sorts of damp, miserable, wet weather, listening to the Top Ten charts for the first time ever. I even got to know lots of the songs, with Mika's 'Grace Kelly' and Rihanna's 'Don't Stop the Music' two that particularly stuck in my head.

By the time 10 a.m. came I would be fine and, physically, I became a lot fitter and stronger as I pushed wheelbarrows, tipped them into skips, lifted stuff lying around the site and helped my dad and the other two men who were on the job.

Out on the site, Dad was very much the boss, and I so admired him for doing this type of work all his life. He's a real grafter and isn't afraid to get his hands dirty, plus, he has an entrepreneurial eye and knows how to take an average house and make it a whole lot better by renovating or extending, making himself a bit of money in the meantime.

I developed a passion for houses from him. He was managing two or three jobs at a time, gutting houses, stripping them, bringing in electricians and making a nice job of it. What he also has is a very sweet tooth and, every day, we'd eat at places like Gregg's or Subway, which, thankfully, was balanced out by all the physical activity we had to pack into our day.

At home in the evenings, Mum would cook dinner and I'd spend a few hours practising new songs and playing the piano until about 11 p.m., when I'd collapse into bed, ready to sleep so I'd be able to get up in the morning for work a little more easily. I'd stopped playing the accordion for a while and was focusing on my voice and piano-playing, and

I was very lucky in that we had by now our own music room at the back of the house, where there was a drum kit, keyboards, a piano, Jake's guitar and fiddle, a concertina and Kiara's whistles.

Out there I could practise melodies and learn new songs for my pub gigs which, mercifully, were starting to pick up on the weekends. By St Patrick's Day I was playing to about four hundred people at the Liffey Bar, where I'd started out playing to only ten. The bar was so stuffed that I could hardly get my gear in past the crowd and the door staff were letting fifty people out to let fifty in at a time – it really was bunged!

At the end of the night I was paid £110, which wasn't a lot less than what I'd earned for a full week on the building site, and it was by doing something I loved. To this day, Nicky James always reminds me never to take that for granted, the ability to earn money by doing something I love doing as opposed to doing a job I had to do just to make ends meet. The buzz of being on stage, watching people dance and sing and clap along to your music, was a massive kick for me and a far cry from being out in the cold at 7 a.m. making cement and lifting bricks.

Nan by now was driving a Toyota Avensis, and she continued to help me get to gigs at the weekends while I laboured with my dad and his work team during the week, braving the elements against my will in order to save and invest in more equipment. We'd pack up her car with my PA, my keyboard, my accordion, a mixing desk, stands, lights, leads and a small merchandise case for my CDs and, when Nan braked, every single time, something would fall on our heads! We always said every night that if we sold more than five CDs we'd stop on the way home for a McDonald's, and Nan rose to the challenge, selling her heart out while I sang. I soon earned enough to buy my very first van – a white 1999 Renault Kangu which was eight years old when I bought it for the grand sum of £1,000. I bought it from a guy who was a bit of a wheeler-dealer in cars and vans around the Irish Centre, and it was perfect for the gigs, giving us a bit more space than Nan's car, where we risked severe head injuries at every junction!

What I learned mostly from my dad was the importance of saving and investment to help my business grow into something bigger and better and, after about nine months, I was able to give up the day job and focus on what I loved doing the most. At the age of seventeen and with my own set of wheels, I was ready to take my music career to another level.

9. Into Adulthood

My dream by now was to step up my game from the pub scene and start to break into the Irish market more, with the long-term vision of fronting my own band still very much at the forefront of my plan. Nicky James was still always close by with words of wisdom and a lot of practical advice when I needed him, and soon I was, under his guidance, recording videos to match two of the songs from my album, *Starting Out*.

We chose a beach location in Redcar in the north-east of England to shoot the videos to *Erin Grá Mo Chroí* (the song I'd won the Fleadh with) and the Garth Brooks classic, 'If Tomorrow Never Comes', and we packaged it up with the album to send out to a list of managers we'd our eye on who were big on the Irish scene.

Nicky was the closest thing I had to a manager at the time, but he didn't want to commit to my long-term plans, due to personal circumstances in his own life, however he wasn't afraid to invest a bit of time to help me get to the next stage. We made a shortlist of four Irish managers – Henry Mc-Mahon, who managed Jimmy Buckley; Sean McGrade, who managed many of the most successful showbands; Big Tom's manager, Kevin McCooey; and Willy Carty, who looked after Mike Denver.

I was excited at the prospect of hearing what these very well-respected managers had to say about me and my music, but I was also very busy and becoming more and more established on the English scene, with four or five gigs now coming in every week. My Kangoo van had been upgraded to a brand-new Renault which I thought was the bees' knees, not realizing it was in fact a disability vehicle(!), and I had my eye on a transit van which I was planning on buying very soon. I was starting to see some familiar faces turning up to gig after gig after gig so, all in all, I was happy with how things were going in the UK, but a move into the Irish market would have been the icing on the cake.

I waited with bated breath for what they would say.

'What age is he?' asked Willy Carty, the only one of the four to give a response to what Nicky and I had sent out. It was disappointing that the others didn't come back to us, but Willy Carty knew his stuff and Mike Denver was probably the hottest young star on the scene at the time.

'He's seventeen,' said Nicky. 'He lives in Liverpool, but he's prepared to travel. What do you think of him?'

'He's really good, a lovely singer,' said Willy. 'I really love his voice, but the problem is that it would take at least a hundred grand to set him up over here with a band and a van and then, after all that, what if he gets homesick and decides to pack it all in?'

Homesick? I *was* very young, and I suppose we hadn't even thought of that ... and all that money? I was deflated and disappointed. How could they not know how much I wanted it? I wouldn't be homesick, I was sure of that. Or was I?

As a stranger who had no idea of my drive, ambition or personality, Willy Carty had a fair point, as I was very young to pack up and move to Ireland, but the rejection stung nonetheless. The reality was that I probably wasn't as ready as I thought I was to make such a move, so I tried to pull myself together, licked my wounds and focused on filling the diary at home in England, moving from pubs to bigger social clubs, then from bigger social clubs to country clubs, and the bookings kept coming in.

The word soon got around, and the net widened in England as we continued to push the CD *Starting Out*, and after the pain of rejection from the Irish managers, there was still a rainbow to be found when, in February 2008, just a few months before my eighteenth birthday, I was invited by Paddy Cowan, managing director of the *Irish World* newspaper, to the prestigious *Irish World* Awards, the very last of its kind to be held at the famous Galtymore dance hall in Cricklewood, London.

The *Irish World* newspaper is the biggest voice of the Irish community living in Britain and has been for the last thirty years and, each year in February, everyone who's anyone from Irish sport, arts and music is invited along for a star-studded evening of entertainment where some of the best are recognized in categories such as Best Country Star and Best Newcomer.

I'll always remember that night and what doors it opened up for me. The Galtymore was an iconic venue, with its high ceilings, crystal chandeliers and all the stories of romance that oozed from its walls.

If the walls of the Galtymore could talk, they could tell so many stories, as it was so much more than just a dancehall for the Irish diaspora. It was a 'home from home', a place to bump into other Irish people on the weekends, a place to dance the night away to the music from the Irish country and showband scene and, all through the twentieth century, in pre-Ryanair times when people couldn't just jump on a plane and pop home for the weekend, it was a godsend to those who missed the Emerald Isle. So that night, when its owner Michael Burns told me at the *Irish World* Awards that it was due to close in May of that year, I felt it was truly the end of an era.

'We're looking for another support act to Big Tom, who is

going to headline the big closing night,' Michael told me. 'Would you be interested in coming along for, say, a forty-five-minute slot?'

Would I *what*? Needless to say, I was shocked and delighted at the very idea of it, and Nan was ecstatic when I told her the news. She used to dance to Joe Dolan at the Galtymore throughout her younger years, so she understood just how big a deal it was to be invited to sing on the closing night.

Best of all, the event was to be held on the night of my eighteenth birthday, 28 May 2008, and as a young musician who wanted to grasp every single opportunity that came my way, I couldn't have asked for a better way to begin my journey into adulthood.

The big night came around and the excitement levels were turned up to the max as me, my mum and dad and Nan and Grumps got all dressed up for the occasion. We'd met a lovely couple on the cruise, Eoin and Carol, who lived in London, and again at the *Irish World* Awards, and they kindly invited all five of us to stay with them. Eoin is no longer with us, unfortunately, though we do still keep in touch with Carol, who comes along to my gigs now. I'll never forget their kindness that night when they allowed us to stay.

I wore an exceptionally embarrassing frilled silver waistcoat which was absolutely awful, but I only have myself to blame for my terrible dress sense back then. I really deserved to be called out by the fashion police!

This was all set to be the biggest crowd I'd ever played to, and my wee van was packed to the rafters with an extra PA in case I needed it. There were to be 2,500 people in the place and, on such an iconic occasion, I wanted to make sure I could be heard properly so I borrowed extra sound equipment just to be certain, though I needn't have bothered, as Big Tom's crew let me plug into theirs. A band called The

Murphys took to the stage and then it was my turn, just me and my keyboard, and I got stuck into a more upbeat country set that had the floor packed with dancers.

I was in my glory, truly pinching myself that I was on stage in the Galtymore, warming up the crowd for Big Tom on the closing night of the country's most famous dance hall. This night was going to go down in history and there I was, playing my own part in it.

I met the now late Big Tom for the first time that night, and I was in awe of how someone who had enjoyed such a lengthy career was still packing in the crowds – what an honour to perform before such a living legend of Irish country music!

I ended up singing not for the planned forty-five minutes but for twice as long, and when I came off stage I felt like I could burst with the thrill of it all. People were asking my name, they were complimenting me on my set and, when I got chatting to Big Tom's manager Kevin McCooey, one of the men Nicky and I had approached not long before, I was hoping he would have some new words of encouragement.

'You're doing well on your own,' he told me. 'You don't need all the expenses and headaches that come with running your own band, believe me.'

I couldn't believe that he had said the exact same thing as Johnny McEvoy had said before. There seemed to be huge costs involved in what I had my heart set on doing, and it didn't look like anyone other than me thought it was such a good idea in any case.

After the highs of the Galtymore, it was back to the drawing board, and Nicky decided we should record a new album that reflected my more upbeat country set which had gone down such a storm in my latest very high-profile performances in London.

My parents threw me an eighteenth-birthday party at Christ the King Parish Hall, where a three-piece live band called Texas Gun from Scotland entertained about two hundred of us, but I often joke that it was more like a sixtieth-birthday party than an eighteenth, as it was full of people who came to my gigs, who were all so much older than me. Nan helped out with the catering, of course, and Mum and Dad got me an accordion-shaped chocolate cake, which was really lovely – it even had my name on it and I was touched that they had gone to so much effort. Jake and Kiara performed their party piece with Jake on fiddle, and Kiara sang her favourite song, 'Love Me' by Colin Rae. Even Grumps had his bit of the limelight when he wowed the guests with a rendition of 'Are You Lonesome Tonight?'

Back in work mode, I needed to keep up the momentum, to keep building on my Galtymore and *Irish World* Awards success, so, never being one to rest on my laurels, I headed back to Redcar Studios and to John Taylor, where my second album, *On the Road*, was born.

It was around this time that I came across a London lady called Gill Marseilles who would help me make the next move into furthering my career. Gill followed all the showbands and she really knew her stuff, so she took a copy of my new album, which featured some much more country sounds, including George Strait covers and Mick Hanley's 'Past the Point of Rescue', which was made famous by Hal Ketchum in the early nineties, and began distributing it out to anyone she thought would listen.

It was Nicky's idea to record a range of songs that reflected the live set I now had such a good grasp of, and, when Gill sent the CD to a contact she had in the Donegal radio station Highland Radio, the DJ Stephen Lynch began to play tracks from it every day for about six months. I bought myself that new transit van which I'd had my eye on for so long, kept my head down and kept pushing the songs and gigs in every way I could, not knowing that, over in Ireland, Stephen Lynch was about to invite me to an event in a little town called Buncrana that would bring me into the same room as someone who would help me make my biggest dream come true. But, first, I would find myself on stage in Ireland for the very first time, accidentally – and that was thanks to Ireland's Queen of Country Music, Philomena Begley.

10. Ireland's Call

Gill Marseilles continued to softly introduce me to as many Irish acts as possible in a live capacity as Highland Radio continued to show an interest in my music, and so I observed closely many of the greats, including Mike Denver, Susan McCann and, of course, Philomena Begley.

I was in the front row at the Abbey Hotel in Donegal with Gill when my most memorable concert with Philomena happened, and it's one that has stuck with me, since it was the first time I ever performed to a country audience on stage in Ireland.

I'd seen Philomena in concert before a few times in Liverpool, and she always brought the house down (she still does!), so there I was, sitting with Gill and minding my own business, when suddenly I became the focus of her attention.

'What's a young lad like you doing here?' she asked me. 'Has an older woman ever shown you a good time?'

Needless to say, my face went pink with embarrassment as the audience erupted in laughter and applause.

'He's a singer!' someone shouted from the audience. 'Get him up!'

Philly has always been known to be up for the craic, so she invited me on stage, where I sang the Keith Whitley hit 'Don't Close Your Eyes' with her live band, which was a truly magical experience, especially when I saw the look on Philomena's face.

'I wasn't expecting that,' she said to me, and then to the audience, 'Will we ask him to sing another one?'

The audience responded with a standing ovation and I

was delighted when the promoter asked me to sing a couple more songs later, during Mike Denver's set. I sang 'Save the Last Dance for Me' and 'Country Roads', again getting a fantastic reaction.

After the show, everyone was asking for pictures and autographs and Philomena came over to me, still bemused at how well the audience had received my impromptu set.

'What's your plans?' Philomena asked me. 'You've got a real talent there. Congratulations.'

I told her, as I told anyone who asked me, that I really wanted to start a band and more or less do what she was doing, and she wished me well in my adventure. It was certainly a night to remember, and Philomena has been very supportive ever since.

Little did I know that night but my big dream was just around the corner, and it was Stephen Lynch of Highland Radio who can be credited with putting me in the same room as John Farry, who would help me make that all-important move of relocating to Ireland and setting up the country band I'd wanted for so long.

Stephen was organizing a benefit concert to be held in Buncrana on 4 May 2009 with guests including Louise Morrissey, Gene Stuart, the Ryan Turner backing band and more, and with the reaction he was getting from playing my new country album on his radio show, he thought I might fit the bill also.

The event was to be held at the Inishowen Gateway Hotel so off I set to Ireland again, with Gill Marseilles, excited to see what opportunities might come my way but not knowing at all what really lay in store.

John Farry is a singer/songwriter from County Fermanagh who was also on the bill that night after being invited to perform a song he wrote called 'Mother's Birthday Song', which was also enjoying some airplay on Stephen's show. John had played in many bands down the years but was best known for his 1997 success in Eurovision when his song 'Mysterious Woman' came in second place. Another of his songs, 'Summertime in Ireland', was Daniel O'Donnell's first number-one hit in Ireland. John has also penned hit songs for Brendan Quinn, Mick Flavin and Ray Lynam, so his finger was really on the pulse when it came to the Irish country scene and songwriting.

As I took to the stage, what I didn't realize was that John Farry was watching me closely, not with a songwriting hat on but with a much more exciting proposal in mind. About six months before the Buncrana gig, John had crossed paths with a top country promoter at the time, another Northern man called James McGarrity, who was well known for keeping an eye on country breakthrough acts as well as organizing and promoting up-and-coming music festivals such as the UTV Countryfest. He and John, who met through a mutual friend, had discussed the possibility of talent-spotting a fresh, new, young country singer who would take the Irish country scene by storm. They had a few people in mind but had their eyes and ears open for anyone who might be what they were looking for.

'I was sitting in the audience that night in Buncrana,' John recalls, 'when this fresh-faced young lad, aged about eighteen or nineteen, stepped on to and swallowed up the stage, blowing everyone else on the bill, with all due respect, out of the water. He just simply stole the show. For me, what I couldn't figure out was how such a diminutive young lad had such a big voice that defied his years. I was totally gobsmacked.

'James and I had travelled to Nashville not long before that and we'd discussed the Irish country scene in great depth. I was a songwriter, he was a promoter and we reckoned, if we put our heads together, we could come up with something magic if we found the right person. Mike Denver was the name on everyone's lips and our mission after that conversation was to find the "new Mike Denver", if you like.'

John left the function room after my performance, having asked a few questions to suss out what my game plan was, and it wasn't hard for him to find out. I wanted a band. I wanted to break the Irish market. I was ready and waiting to be discovered.

'What do you think of that lad, Nathan Carter?' he asked Ryan Turner, who had been in charge of the band that night. 'He looks like he might do well?'

Ryan Turner had replied, 'It depends who gets him,' and John knew he had to act fast. He went outside immediately and phoned James McGarrity.

'I think I've found our man,' he told James. 'This guy is the real deal. Looks good, sounds even better and seems like a nice lad.'

'Go and talk to him quickly,' said James and, before long, John was shaking my hand and introducing himself.

'What are your plans?' John asked me.

'I want to start my own band,' I told him, and waited for the usual response about me being better off on my own, about the extortionate and impossible costs involved, about the never-ending politics, the egos, and all the other challenges involved. I expected John, just like the others before him, to try and talk me out of it. But he didn't.

'We'd love to talk to you more about putting a band around you. What do you think? Would you be up for it?'

I took a deep breath.

'Yes . . . yes, I would,' I said to John with a beaming smile, and we exchanged contact details, agreeing to meet up very soon to see if we could progress things further.

John, James, Nicky and I met a few days later in the White Horse Hotel in Eglinton, near the Derry City airport, where we talked through the logistics of the common goal that we all seemed to have in mind. I would move to Ireland, where John and James would form a company around me and my music; they'd find me the best band they could, put together a marketing strategy, work up some new material and some launch events and break into the Irish country-music market with a bang.

I was so glad to have Nicky there with me to hear what they were saying and to get a second opinion. I hadn't even reached my nineteenth birthday yet and, even though I may have thought I knew it all, I still had a lot to learn when it came to contracts and plans, so Nicky listened carefully and, although we both liked what we heard, it was time to take the two prospective managers to Liverpool to talk to the people whose opinion I respected the most – my parents.

A couple of weeks later John and James arrived at our family home in Liverpool, so that, as John put it, we could see the whites of everybody's eyes. We went for lunch, where my parents discussed the boys' aspirations for me and how they were going to break me as a new artist in a very well-established and very competitive market. Dad, being a businessman in his own right, asked plenty of questions, and we left the meeting with a view of a contract being drawn up in a bid to keep all our best interests at heart. Just as those managers had told me before, there was going to be a fair bit of financial investment involved to get this whole project off the ground, so it was important that everyone's needs were well looked after and respected.

The only thing that we disagreed on, in a light-hearted way, was my name and my appearance. With the huge success of Mike Denver, John thought it might be an idea to put

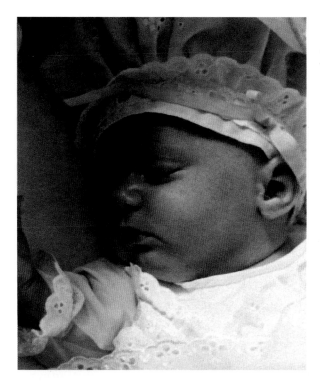

Just having a nap …

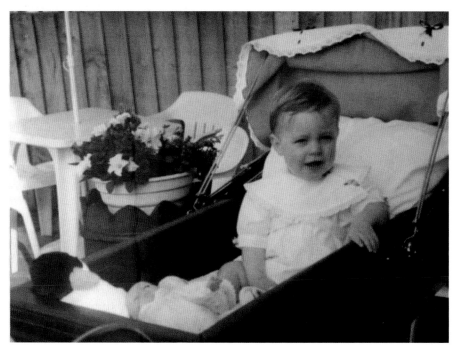

Chillin' in the garden …

Nan, Grumps and me

Singing with Daniel in our living room … 'D.O.D.' and I, our first duet
together …

Grumps teaching me how it's done

Fiddlin' around on Christmas Day

Maybe I should have played the drums …

Dad and me … my first day as an apprentice

Me, Jake and Kiara enjoying a day at the beach

My first home gig! With an audience of Nan and Kiara

Black-tie affair: Merseyside and Cheshire Young Achiever Awards, 2003, voted Best Musician

Performance in Windsor Castle Chapel: myself as head chorister in the St Francis Xavier Boys' Choir

Me and my other nan, Amana Carter

Kiara's Holy Communion day, with Jake, Mum and Dad

Me and my uncle John Carter at my dad's fortieth-birthday party

Family fancy-dress at Dad's fortieth-birthday party

I'm a one-man band ... playing the keyboards in Leeds Irish Centre

Leeds Irish Centre: Jake on fiddle and Kiara on melodeon

me in a white suit and cowboy hat and change my name to Johnny Carter to suit the country scene. I said no, of course, and we still laugh about that now, though we did compromise when he got me to wear a silver suit!!

The contract was pushed around for quite a while before we were all happy with it, but soon we had a written agreement that we could all work to. I was really keen not to be just an employee of the company John and James were proposing. I wanted to have a strong say in the decision-making process of everything that my career involved and, even though I knew I could never do everything myself if I wanted to play on bigger stages and to bigger audiences, I'd learned quite a bit from gigging and recording so far and I was keen not to throw that all away and become a puppet to the industry – an industry which I craved and loved but which I knew could also make mincemeat of you if you got into the wrong hands.

My dad and I studied the contract and made the changes we felt necessary to be sure it was exactly what I was happy with and, eventually, I signed up.

I'd waited for what felt like a very long time to find a manager (or, in this case, managers) who were as eager as I was to put together a band, not to mention a 'brand', and to boost my music career to the next level but, even so, I wanted to make sure that, now that it was all happening for real, I was going into this agreement with my eyes wide open.

A manager must be trustworthy, they must be financially on the ball, and be at least two steps ahead of the game when it comes to marketing and publicity and securing tour dates at the best venues. A manager will at various times have to be an artist's closest friend, a confidant, a coach, a mentor, a psychologist, a stylist, a driver, a shopper, a sparring partner, a cheerleader, an expert in a crisis.

Now I'd finally found mine, I had the overwhelming prospect of leaving behind everything I'd ever known, and I hoped I wouldn't be throwing the baby out with the bath water with my big decision to move to Ireland.

I asked my dad if he thought I was doing the right thing.

'We both know how much you want this,' he told me. 'And nothing in life has to be for ever. If it doesn't work out, at least you can always say you gave it your best shot.'

I could feel the excitement bubble inside me.

'Are you sure you're okay with this, Mum?'

Mum shrugged and smiled.

'We're right behind you, love, but it's entirely up to you whether you want to go through with it. We'll be with you every step of the way.'

I looked at my dad for a final word of reassurance.

'At the end of the day,' he said, 'what do you have to lose? Give it three years and, if it doesn't work out, you can always come back home.'

I knew exactly what he meant, and I didn't have any room for second thoughts, as it was what I'd wanted so badly, but, naturally, in my head, I did start to go over everything that I'd be giving up to chase my dream.

The transit van I'd just bought for myself, which was a huge step up from the Renault Kangoo, not to mention Nan's trusty old Honda Civic, where all the gear used to fall on our heads every time she braked. I'd be leaving the regular gigs at the Liffey Bar, where everybody knew my name; the Irish centres, where I had now become a star attraction and could always pull a crowd; the memories and the comfort of knowing that Nan would be in the audience no matter where I'd go, with her little merchandise case, and that when I looked down, I'd see her fixing her hair to signal to me that everything would be okay if I felt nervous or anxious at all. I wouldn't have my mum and dad to go home to at night or Jake and Kiara to play music with and to encourage when they felt like giving up their own music or to referee when they had one of their rows over something totally trivial, like getting Lucozade instead of milk; the craic with Grumps and his bewilderment when Nan landed back with some random item from the shops or, much worse, on his credit card, or his party piece of 'Are You Lonesome Tonight?', where he'd replace the proper lyrics with 'Are your knickers too tight?', just to make me laugh on stage; I wouldn't have any of the regular gigs I was out doing four or five nights a week and, for a nineteen-year-old, earning a fairly decent wage for it.

I was going to a place where almost no one knew my name, never mind leaving behind the things I was used to and held most close to me.

I was going to leave my whole life behind for the country that I'd always felt so attached to but now realized I knew very little about.

This time, I wasn't going to Ireland to compete in the Fleadh or to stay in a caravan and laugh about how uncomfortable it was, knowing it was only going to be for a few days and then I'd be home in my own cosy bed with enough memories to keep me going until the next time.

This was completely different altogether. This was a leap in the dark, a leap of faith. This was what dreams were made of, and I was determined that I would try and make it work.

I was finally going to Ireland to form my own band. I'd never been so excited, or scared, in my whole life.

11. Leaving of Liverpool

Before the contracts with my new management company were even signed and before I'd packed my bags to actually move to Ireland, I found myself under the care of Jonathan Owens at Spout Studios in Granard, County Longford, where I was brought to record my first single for the Irish market, 'Games People Play', a Grammy-winning song by the late American artist Joe South.

Jonathan Owens was top of the tree when it came to recording country music in Ireland, he was at the front of the queue and kept up to date with excellent production ideas, plus, he proved very easy to work with, which helped me relax into my first recording session.

The plan was to have the single recorded even before we had established a band and before I moved over to Ireland so that we had something new that would promote the image we wanted ready and waiting for when we'd hit the road – very clever thinking and a way of hitting the ground running.

'Games People Play' was an ideal song to launch with as it had a sing-along title which we adapted to give it a more country vibe and a rounded, happy feel that would fit the image I was looking for, and I enjoyed laying down the track with Jonathan in this all-new environment.

While I was busy putting the song down in the studio, my new management were sourcing band personnel and logistical stuff – a vehicle, for one thing – and they had the job of finding a PA system, which we scraped together with the budget we had allowed, and, at the same time, John was working on some original songs for my future recordings.

Sourcing the band personnel was the most important task, of course, and they came up against the usual scenario, where the musicians they wanted were already in comfortable jobs with established musicians and were reluctant to take a gamble on a newcomer like me. But soon they found a musical director, Jim McVeigh, who agreed to come out of retirement to find the right people to come on the road with me, and progress was quickly made.

We mailed the single 'Games People Play' out to Irish radio stations in CD format and waited in hope for some airplay as we paddled away under the surface, trying to pull the whole project together. Some radio stations played it, some didn't, and sometimes it came to calling in favours in a case of 'It's not what you know, it's who you know' to try and give the song a chance. We set up some radio and press interviews and prepared some glossy leaflets with my face and name on them – the first of their kind on the Irish country scene – announcing that I was the next big thing and giving details of the new single. They went out to events promoters, country-music venues, the Irish media and all of the radio stations across the country, so many people in the industry knew my name and what I was being promoted as before they'd heard me even sing a note.

A buzz was beginning to hum around the circuit and, with the help of a few favours, that hum turned into a lilt as people started hearing my song on the radio and the name Nathan Carter was drip-fed into people's cars and homes and workplaces, anywhere there was a radio that played country music.

Meanwhile, back in the real world, I was preparing to leave home for the very first time and I knew that, behind it all, even though she knew it was for the best, my mum was breaking her heart at the idea of saying goodbye to her eldest son. She would no longer see me every day. I had been fairly spoiled at home and had no idea how to cook or clean, never mind use a washing machine, so the practicalities, let alone the emotional side of moving out, were tricky enough to get my head around.

Nan had pulled out her little black book of contacts and had managed to find me a room at a house in a place called Bridge End, the home of a couple called Ann and Jim McClay and their daughter, Sonia. Nan knew the McClay family through an aromatherapy company she was then working for in her spare time and which had taken her on all sorts of exotic and exciting trips, including a holiday to Hawaii, which, of course, didn't surprise anyone, as Nan was always up to something exciting and forever on the go!

The McClay home was a cosy detached bungalow and there were a lot of farm animals around – pigs and hens, ducks, dogs and sheep – which was a huge change to the bright lights of Liverpool, where I'd grown up, but perhaps the most unique feature of my new residence was that, geographically, the front garden was in County Derry and the back garden was in County Donegal! How's that for a cross-border challenge? Whether you dealt in euros or pounds sterling was determined by which door you left the house from!

Soon, the big day to leave my home in my beloved Liverpool arrived and, as I sat on my bed, looking around my room, I remember questioning myself as to whether or not I was doing the right thing at all. I couldn't look at Mum, who was so upset as we packed up my transit van, for fear it might set us both off, so I focused on piling in all my stuff so tightly that you couldn't get a mouse into it if you tried. All my clothes, all my music equipment – my whole life, really – was packed into that van, and I just kept on avoiding Mum's face in case I made her worse. I knew she was trying so hard not to cry. I later found out that, having sailed across with me to Bridge End, the whole way back to Liverpool Mum had bawled her eyes out, worrying about who was going to look out for me and what I'd do if I felt scared or lonely over in Ireland all by myself. I may have been nineteen years old, but I was still her baby, and I'm so glad I didn't know how upset she really was at the time or I'd never have settled, with me worrying about her worrying about me, but then that's what families are for, isn't it?

The reality once I got settled in meant that I had very little time to think about what I might be missing back at home in Liverpool. It was straight to work now that the band was set up and a list of dates filled my diary so it really was a case of being thrown in at the deep end.

I moved across to Ireland in January 2010 and the months before that, since our first meeting in May the year before, had been very busy, recording and promoting the single, recruiting the band, and now, here I was, just about to dip my toe into the famous Irish country-music scene. I hadn't a clue what to expect.

It was 10 January that year when I met my band at the Greenvale Hotel in Cookstown, County Tyrone, for our first rehearsal for our very first gig, which would be held at the same venue on 21 January. It was an event that was planned to launch me on to the country scene officially.

Jim McVeigh was a keyboard player and musical director who had just left the Dominic Kirwan band, and was perhaps looking into softly retiring from the music business, but he was interested enough in what we were planning and agreed to come on board as MD and to get the band together. He found a drummer in Gareth Lowry from Castlederg,

County Tyrone; a bass player in Jimmy Hendry from Sion Mills, also in County Tyrone; Seamus Rooney from Portaferry, County Down, on rhythm guitar; and Stevie Hamilton from Banbridge, County Armagh, on lead and steel guitar.

I arrived at the Greenvale with butterflies in my tummy, overwhelmed at meeting my very own band for the first time. All these men, apart from the drummer, Gareth, who I figured was around my own age, had been playing country music in many bands for many years and I got the impression they thought I was a bit wet behind the ears, a young lad from Liverpool who was brand new to such a well-established scene.

I'd previously met Jim McVeigh about a week before the event and we'd gone through a set list, but when it came to the first rehearsal I was very nervous to be singing in front of these strangers, some of whom had been playing music for over thirty years.

Everyone was welcoming and friendly, and perhaps even a little bit surprised for the better once we got started and the sound we were after came to life. They saw that I really did know my way around a piano and an accordion and could hold a tune, as opposed to just being an unprepared, fresh-faced youngster that stood before them. We worked through a set list of dance lovers' favourites to suit our anticipated crowd and, after a second rehearsal the following day, we were ready to go and make our big debut. It had been well hyped up, thanks to people like Hugo Duncan of BBC Radio Ulster, Paul Claffey of Midwest Radio and Pio McCann of Highland Radio, who were now playing my single and adding to the speculation and mystery of this new act on the country circuit.

The audience on the big night was made up of three hundred invited guests, all carefully selected from the Irish radio, press and the general music scene – venue owners and pro-moters, for example – and, despite a few blips on sound, we got a great reaction overall.

I was like a child in a toyshop on the night, chatting to everyone who came along, and I enjoyed meeting new faces from the business, all of whom wanted to share their advice with me on what to sing, what not to sing and all sorts of other tips on how to make the most of the opportunity that was coming my way. The night was a great success, but it was perhaps in a way a glorified taster of what life on the road was all about because, in reality, getting three hundred people to come to your follow-up gigs as an unknown singer from across the sea was a very different story indeed.

Needless to say, it didn't happen overnight and, for a long time, we lost money.

In those days, it was all about filling the diary at least four nights a week to keep the band in regular work. The dance scene in Ireland was our market and it was known that Thursday nights would clear the band costs, if we were lucky, Friday night might be just okay, Saturday was the big one and the night we'd hope to make a bit extra, while Sunday would take a dip again. When it came to getting bookings with the venues across Ireland, the general feeling was that you were only ever as good as your last gig.

The second gig after the launch night in Greenvale was a bit further afield, in Claremorris, County Mayo, and then we travelled across to Dublin to Tailor's Rock, and we carried on from there, not knowing what type of crowds – or lack of crowds – to expect along the way.

These crowds were humble enough in most places, and a lot of nights were tough, but we always believed that we had enough talent, a decent band and we just had to keep sowing seeds to make it happen. The rules of play were that, even if you played to a poor crowd the very first time, most venues would give you a second chance to prove yourself, but the third one was the deal-breaker: if it didn't do well, then they wouldn't have you back. This was pressure, it was real, and I was beginning to understand what those well-respected managers had told me before as to how hard it could sometimes be.

On top of all that, I was definitely missing home. At times, I wondered if I really was as streetwise and confident as I thought I would be in a new country, in a new home and so far away from everything I'd ever known. I rang Mum every single day, which helped, and Ann, who I was staying with, was very kind to me, as was Sonia, who showed me around the neighbourhood. Ann helped me out with washing and ironing and made sure I didn't go hungry so, as well as renting a room from her, I did have some home comforts, which made it a lot easier to be away from Liverpool. My parents came to visit as often as they could, as did Nan and Grumps, but still there were times when I longed for the days when I could see Nan in the audience to reassure me that I was doing well and that everything was going to be okay.

I'd hear her say the words she used to say to me when I was a little boy.

'Was I good, Nan?'

'You're getting better. Keep practising.'

And with that I'd remember how long I'd wished for this to happen. I couldn't let it fail. Never for one moment did I think it *would* fail, even on nights like the one in Slane, County Meath, when we were so excited and were told it was going to be a big crowd. We set up our instruments and PA on stage and even moved chairs to accommodate the anticipated audience. The venue manager was in a bit of a fluster, wondering how he was going to accommodate any more than 120 people and he too was moving chairs and tables to try and make more space. We did our sound check and then waited backstage for the doors to open and the place to fill up with eager punters. And we waited . . . and we waited . . . and we waited, until, eventually, I had to go out to the dance hall on my own and offer all sixteen people who showed up their money back and a promise of tickets to a future gig. It was like a kick in the stomach at the time, but we managed to find some live music elsewhere to entertain us for the evening and after a couple of pints we managed to swallow our pride. It is the only time I remember not going on stage to perform, and to say it was a humbling experience is an understatement. Put it this way, I knew after that never to take anything for granted when it comes to the music industry!

One night in the Hazel Tree Mallow in County Cork also brought us down to earth with a bump. There was very heavy snow on the ground and we were forced into a decision whether or not to play when only fifty-two people turned up, but we managed to get through it and played on, though it was definitely a challenge to keep the spirits up, playing to such a small audience in a big dance hall. And then there was the Tullyglass Hotel in Ballymena, where fifty-six people turned up, so we waited an extra fifteen minutes to go on, hoping that more would turn up, but by the time we went on stage there were only forty-seven!

Another night that stands out from those early days was when we were booked to play a wedding in Spiddal, County Galway, and the guests were lively, to say the least, some of them even offering us cash at the end of the night to play longer and longer and longer into the wee hours – so we never knew what to expect when we'd turn up to perform. It really was like a lucky dip of funny, mad and sometimes, when we lost money, downright sad experiences in those early days.

Despite such a mixture of highs and lows back then, I can't say that we ever had what I'd call a 'bad' gig, so to speak. Every night was a new experience and something that I decided to learn from, whether it was good, or not so good, such as one night in Leitrim, when the sound went off and we had to channel down to just a few outputs from the sound desk, which wasn't complimentary to our music or my vocals, and that's putting it mildly . . .

However, with the band gelling so well behind me, my confidence grew, our set became tighter and we were determined to keep making it better and better, no matter what came our way. If it didn't work out how we expected, we'd just make the most of it, and I learned very quickly how important that old saying 'The show must go on' is. I couldn't afford to take small crowds personally. I couldn't afford it in the *literal* sense, in that the band had to be paid first – that was always a priority – so rain, hail or shine, we kept our show on the road, travelling to dance halls in all corners of the country and hoping that, one day, our magic would light a spark in a very competitive industry where everyone is out to get a slice of the action.

I needed to stand out from the crowd if I was going to make my mark and attract people to my shows. I suppose you could say I needed a unique selling point. Looking back, at the time, I didn't realize that, slowly, the tides were turning in my favour.

12. Turning Twenty-one

My first album in Ireland, *The Way that You Love Me*, and the follow-up, which was called *The Time of My Life*, were very much seedling albums and were totally reflective of the dance scene in Ireland, with a mixture of jives, quicksteps and ballads that could be performed in our live set. That was getting better every time we played, as were the crowds that followed us.

A Nathan Carter gig soon became a stomping ground for hot-blooded young males who were chasing the hot-blooded young females who were chasing the hot-blooded young singer on the stage – and there was the unique selling point we were looking for! This was not something we could take for granted, of course, but it seemed to be the way things were turning for us and, with an impressive repertoire of brand-new songs, some penned by John Farry especially for me and my band, and a mix of country classics that everyone could recognize and sing along to, we began to make our mark wherever we went.

I continued to watch and learn from the greats and, when I was given a support slot on the Country Queens concert tour, which featured American artists such as Billie Jo Spears, Leona Williams and Georgette Jones, as well as Ireland's very own country queen Philomena Begley, it was a perfect opportunity for me to hone my craft. Concerts were a very different environment than the dances, as I would have to talk between songs a lot more and, with all eyes and ears on me, there was nowhere to hide. I soon got the hang of it, even if I was a bit nervous at the start.

'Slow down, Nathan,' said Philomena to me one night in the wings. 'The people in the audience aren't going anywhere. Remember they are here to see you and to listen to you, so just take your time when you're talking and it will all be grand.'

We toured the Northern Irish theatre scene, playing venues such as the Marketplace in Armagh and the Strule in Omagh, and when I bought myself a second-hand petrol-engine Honda Civic 2.5 from my musical director Jim McVeigh, I didn't do the maths. It only did about 25 miles to the gallon, which was totally unsuitable for long distances, especially when one run out was to Cork, which cost me an absolute fortune!

My first proper album launch took place in Enniskillen at a place called the Fort Lodge, nicknamed the Lodge of Love, and we booked in a few well-known singers, such as The Benn Sisters and Robert Mizzell, to add to the bill as special guests, continuing to promote *The Way that You Love Me* at every opportunity. Our formula was to release a new single every three months. This would encourage new radio play, and this would then trickle back on to the walk-up on our live gigs, which meant a rise in numbers all around. It was a good formula, and it kept the airwaves fresh and the listeners interested in hearing more.

We were becoming busier and busier, and my days off were few and far between, which meant that, although I had very little time to think of what might be going on back at home in Liverpool, there were also many occasions when I wasn't able to fly home for such events as family weddings and christenings. I had to really weigh up the knock-on effect of taking a night off – it wasn't just me I had to think of, it was the whole band. I now had a lot of responsibility on my still very young shoulders.

With such pressures and a huge commitment at such a young age, I still needed friends I could call on and, luckily, I made some easily in Ireland. The Benn Sisters, Carrie and Leanne, would chat to me after those early launch events, and I got to know some music fans who would turn up on different occasions, many of whom, among them Cathal Fee, are still close friends now. We all began to hang out together as a group and, later, we'd go on holidays together and catch some music gigs on my rare nights off. Having a circle of friends around my own age made me feel very much at home in Ireland and it was nice to have people to call on when I needed a chat or a friendly face.

I first met fellow country singer Lisa McHugh in the Milford Inn in Donegal, where she was singing on the same bill as Robert Mizzell. I recognized her from her recent appearance on *Glór Tíre*, the TG4 singing talent show.

I fancied her instantly.

Lisa, who is from Glasgow, was in Ireland to pursue a career in country music, just like I was, and I soon found out that we had lots in common, so I approached her and asked for her number. I think she thought it was a bit cheeky, but I wasn't wasting any opportunities. Lisa was living in Letterkenny, which was only half an hour from where I was at the time, and I sent her a few text messages. I have to admit, she wasn't too forthcoming with her replies at first!

I met her again a short while later, at an awards ceremony at the Tullyglass Hotel in Ballymena, and eventually I asked her out on a date to the cinema in Letterkenny. We started to hang out together, and soon we were enjoying a fun-filled romantic relationship, which mainly entailed listening to music – we had very similar tastes: Carrie Underwood, Brad Paisley, The Dixie Chicks; we also shared very similar tastes in food – Chinese, Indian, McDonald's, chip-shop food, and a lot of Subways! Needless to say, we were both a lot heavier then than we are now, due to our unhealthy diet, despite our busy schedules!

As well as a love of junk food and country music, Lisa and I were very focused on our individual careers. I don't think I've ever met anyone as driven and ambitious, and we bounced off each other when it came to discussing our plans for the future. She was appearing at different events as a solo act and I advised her to start up her own band, just like I had, believing that she had the talent and vision to make it work.

In the end, though, around six months later, it was the same shared ambition that made us call it a day on any sort of romance, deciding we were better off as friends after all. We were both very young, and neither of us was looking for anything serious, plus, my career was really taking off by that stage, and it allowed for less and less time to be spent with anyone outside of the band and for doing anything other than being on the road.

Lisa still remains one of my best friends, and we help each other out as much as possible. I still value her advice. She is very good at seeing the bigger picture, she is very strong-minded and has a good ear when I need a friend, which I am very thankful for. I'm lucky to have built a strong circle of people who I can confide in, and Lisa is certainly one of them. She was there when I celebrated my twenty-first birthday party after a gig at the Du Pont club in Derry, when Ann and Jim McClay threw a party at their house for me.

It was a great night, and I was thrilled to bits when my mum and dad arrived, plus all the band, and we partied into the wee hours as I celebrated reaching another important milestone in my personal life.

Meanwhile, professionally, after months and months of slogging away, playing four and five nights a week with my band and targeting radio stations with a range of singles, things were definitely looking up. *Time of My Life* was doing well in the Irish charts and, with the introduction of the popular TV programme *Hot Country* on Sky, making a video to match every single was a brilliant way of attracting new audiences as far away as Scotland and England. I also had an idea to record a live show which we could then distribute on DVD, and we did this at the Burnavon Theatre in Cookstown.

The project cost a lot of money, but we had been investing any profits back into the business and it was a risk I was willing to take. Thankfully, it was one that paid off.

'The DVD is flying off the shelves,' Raymond Stewart from the distributing company Sharpe Music told me on the phone one day when I was driving to a gig in Donegal. 'I've never seen anything like it. It's outselling CDs and it has made the Top Twenty in the Irish charts. This is a real first for a live recording in country music.'

I couldn't believe it. Radio stations began to pick up on its success, with broadcasters such as Hugo Duncan (BBC), Pio McCann (Highland) and Big T of Downtown Radio really championing the tracks, and it began to translate into our audiences, especially in the south of Ireland, where we had been struggling with numbers, despite our growing success in the Northern counties.

John Farry had taken over as manager when James McGarrity parted ways with us, and some of the songs we had recorded were really beginning to catch on. John penned a track about the famous Leitrim ballroom called 'The Rainbow in Glenfarne', and we also wrote our own version of Christy Moore's 'Encore', mentioning every venue we'd played in, which was a great, fun way of highlighting all the fantastic dance halls we'd now frequented.

I played the Mellon and the Bushtown, the Ryandale
  and Cookstown,
I played the famous Rainbow in Glenfarne.
Derrygonnelly, Antrim, Newry, Sligo, Moath,
  and 'Blaney.
And a wild night in Dungiven in a barn.

The king of all venues was the Allingham Arms Hotel in Bundoran, which is thronging at the weekends, with country-music fans from all over, and we longed for the day when we would pack out these venues and see that coveted 'Doors Closed' sign which meant the place was packed to capacity.

As an artist, when you see people coming into a venue and dancing the night away to your music, especially to some of the original tracks you've put together just for the band, it's truly an overwhelming sensation, and what we started to notice was that our audiences were becoming younger and younger – and younger and younger and younger!

Country music, to my own admission, had never really been seen as 'cool', yet here were thirtysomethings, then twenty-somethings, then even eighteen- and nineteen-year-olds coming to our gigs and showing what it was like to really get lost in the music and enjoy a good old-fashioned jive.

'There's magic in this,' John Farry told me one night. 'You have a connection with the audience, something that's hard to put your finger on, but it's there. Whether they're dancing or just sitting down and enjoying the music, you're doing something new, and it's really catching on. There's a buzz. The young people are coming out in their droves. This has never been seen in recent years. It's new.'

From one venue date to the next, we'd notice the audience numbers grow and grow, and I started to be recognized, not particularly in public, but for those who followed country music, my name and my face, as well as my music, were becoming more and more popular. People were now singing along to our own songs, especially an upbeat jive called 'One for the Road', which had become a bit of an anthem for us to play at the end of the night. It was the perfect finishing song, suggesting that there was always time for more, and whenever I heard the dancers in front of me belt out the lyrics, the feeling was electric.

'One for the Road', which was written by John Farry, was a kind of breakthrough song in many ways, and it brought us a lot more airplay, with its catchy sing-along chorus and upbeat message. We shot a video for the song in Drum Manor Forest in Cookstown, County Tyrone, with filmmaker Mick Bracken, and another video was shot at Lough Eske in Donegal for a song called 'The Dancer', which also helped to sell the albums. As social media became a more frequent way of communicating to our audiences, we were able to share these videos, which again kept people interested and, it seemed, wanting more.

The days of playing to only a handful of people hadn't been that long ago, but here we were, witnessing something that was beyond even our wildest dreams. Every night we were out, it just seemed to get bigger and bigger.

One Friday night we were playing the Mellon Country Inn in Omagh when, at 10.30 p.m., not long before we were due to go onstage, our then tour manager Brendan Donnelly came in to me to break the good news we'd been wishing and hoping for.

'There's seven hundred people in, Nathan,' he told me. 'They've had to put up the full-house sign. You've packed the place to capacity. Well done.'

I couldn't speak.

'Packed to capacity?' I said finally. 'Really? Are you serious?'

I was gobsmacked. Seven hundred people and the full-house sign! Wow. I just couldn't believe it.

'And that's not all,' said Brendan. 'There's another one hundred or so waiting outside, hoping to get in. It's mad. They're going crazy for you out there.'

My heart was thumping in my chest, and the first thing I did was ring my mum back in Liverpool.

'You'll never believe it, Mum,' I told her. 'We've sold out a dance hall for the very first time! There's even people waiting outside, wanting to get in. Can you believe it?'

My mum was elated and totally shocked. Her voice shook in response.

'You deserve it, love,' she told me with glowing pride. 'You deserve this so, so much. Embrace it and enjoy every moment. We are all so proud of you, Nathan. Me and your dad are so proud.'

I went on stage that night with a new feeling of invigoration and pure joy, and we rocked the place until after 1 a.m., churning out song after song from the two albums and the live DVD, all of which had brought us such a diverse audience who knew all the words to every song.

'I can't get over so many young people turning up at the dances,' said Nan when she came to visit and attended one of the gigs. Nan would visit me at least every two months, so she had witnessed the massive change that had happened organically over the past two years. 'Where on earth are they all coming from?'

The promoters who worked with us were astounded by this too, and it was only just beginning. The same venue on our return a while later was filled again to capacity with seven hundred people, only this time, instead of one hundred people waiting outside to get in, there were four hundred!

'We've never seen anything like this before,' the staff at

the Mellon Country Inn used to say to me. 'By 9.30 p.m. we have to close the doors. This has never happened before.'

The Newry and Mourne Country Inn was the same. The Tullyglass Hotel in Ballymena, where we once played to those forty-seven people, drew an even bigger crowd, with 1,600 people in one night and another two hundred outside. At the Ryandale in Moy, County Tyrone, people were trying to climb over the high fences and mesh wire to get in through the back doors. It really was absolutely crazy!

But we never took our foot off the pedal. We never took it for granted. I was constantly updating social media as well as promoting our gigs in the more traditional ways, like newspapers and radio, and all of this kept up the connection with the ever growing members of our audiences, who were getting bigger in number and younger in age. I just kept wondering when it would all end. It was like I was living in a bubble and I didn't want it to ever burst, so I just kept recording and trying to come up with more and more ideas to keep everyone interested in what we were going to do next.

But I could never have anticipated what was coming up. The bubble was set to float even higher, and all because – would you believe? – a ringtone on my friend Aisling Fee's phone caught my ear. It was a song that I'd never heard before, but there was something about it that made me want to investigate further, so I asked Aisling what the name of the song was. She suggested I record it, but I wasn't so sure at first.

And then I looked it up on YouTube, where I heard those very famous words loud and clear.

Rock me, Mama, like a –

Yes, that's it. Like a wagon wheel. I thought you might know the rest . . . and I bet you're singing it now . . .

Rock me, Mama, like a wagon wheel.

Things were set to get a whole lot crazier.

13. 'Wagon Wheel'

At its best, it's been viewed over 6 million times on YouTube, and it led to a number-one album of the same title in 2012. At its worst, it's been labelled 'psychological torture' and has been on a list of banned wedding songs (which makes me laugh – 'Galway Girl' is on that list too). But there's one thing for sure – my unexpected cover version of Bob Dylan's 'Wagon Wheel' was a groundbreaking force in my career that can never be called forgettable.

The catchy refrain of 'Hey, Mama, rock me' is basically inescapable. It's definitely one of those songs that sticks in your head – not bad, considering it originated when Bob Dylan was just messing around when he was writing his twelfth album, a soundtrack to a movie about Billy the Kid back in 1973. The song, about a gambler who decides to leave his old life behind, became famous when a band called the Old Crow Medicine Show put Dylan's chorus and melody together and released it in 2001, and it was this version that I had heard playing on my friend's phone.

We recorded the song with Jonathan Owens at Spout Studio in Granard and, when it came in at a lengthy four minutes and twenty seconds, we initially thought it might be too long for radio play.

Jonathan recalls, 'I remember Nathan coming in with the song, which was to be the last recording for the album. We'd been looking for a single, but nothing had jumped out so far, and when he played "Wagon Wheel" to me I instantly recognized it, knowing the Old Crow Medicine Show version was

96

doing the rounds in student circles, and I'd also heard it on holiday.

'While the Old Crow version certainly had something, it was time for Nathan and me to put our heads together and see how it could be adapted into being more along the lines of what Nathan Carter fans would like and what Nathan liked himself, so I sat down at the piano, Nathan lifted the guitar and we got started.

'We were looking for a big, bouncy sound and wanted to give it a very distinctive opening, so we added in the drum fill that you hear at the beginning, only to find that the song was over four minutes long, which wasn't ideal for radio play,' says Jonathan.

'We trimmed and trimmed the song as much as we could, having added in the fiddle, banjo and accordion to give a nod to the trad/country feel we were after, and it all just came together so naturally. We raised the tempo so that it was a song that could be danced to and not just a clap-along, and put in a funky radio-friendly element, something cool and a bit risqué, perhaps, compared to the more traditional country sound that was out there. I'd noticed this was happening in America, but it hadn't really made its way here yet, and it totally worked.

'There is no real formula for producing a hit – it either happens or it doesn't – but with all the little artefacts (the accordion, the drumbeat, the fiddle, the banjo, the big, catchy chorus), it felt like something was happening. John Farry had a listen. He loved it. There was magic in the air, and I suppose we can now say the rest is history.'

'Wagon Wheel' was sent out to radio in the same way as all my previous singles, but this one – well, the big difference was that it appealed to everyone from four-year-old children to eighty-something grannies. They were all requesting it on their local and national stations. In fact, 'Wagon Wheel' was on people's lips before it even got to radio as, somehow, it became a popular request on jukeboxes, with wedding DJs and listeners knowing the song without even knowing it was me singing it, but soon both my name and the song were matched up and it began to catch fire.

With every good song, we needed a good video, so for this one we hired in the expertise of Dungannon video-grapher and director Donovan Ross, who met us on the beach at Rossnowlagh in County Donegal, a location we chose for mainly logistical reasons, in that we knew a lot of people who had houses near the beach, we could drive on to it, and it's a very pretty spot for the outdoor, carefree atmosphere we wanted to go along with the song.

When brainstorming for the video, our then fiddle player Matt McGrenaghan, drummer Gareth Lowry and I had imagined a beach, a barbecue, an old boxed piano and other instruments and some friends gathered around a campfire – oh, and a good old VW campervan that looked both cool and retro at the same time, which we borrowed from Gareth's cousin.

I found the piano online and couldn't believe that it was for sale just up the road from me in Tempo. I'd been looking for a very old, battered piano that wasn't up to much so that we could set it on fire at the end (I know, how rock 'n' roll!) and, lo and behold, there it was, only a few miles away. However, when we went to pick it up, we had to take the back of the piano off and dismantle it so that we could lift it, as parts of it were made of really old cast iron. It ended up taking us a whole three hours, which felt like a day's work on its own, we were so exhausted after it.

I convinced almost everyone in my circle of friends in Enniskillen to come along for the craic and, if you look closely, you will spot Johnny Gallagher of the famous Boxtie band from Bundoran, and my manager, John Farry, was in the background, cooking up burgers on a barrel which was cut in half to create a makeshift barbecue.

On the day of the location 'reccy' when we went up to Rossnowlagh to check out where we would set everything up, Donovan managed to lock his keys in his car, and his wife, Teresa, had to travel all the way from Dungannon, a good two-hour drive, to rescue him. Donovan was fun and creative to work with and, when it came to the day of the shoot, everything came together very nicely and we all had a blast.

Despite the blue skies that are shown in the video for 'Wagon Wheel', the day of the shoot was very cold and we had to grit our teeth and get on with it, trying to put across an upbeat, lively and summery feel. The end result, though simple and maybe a bit cheesy, worked for what we needed it for – to get more airplay on the growing number of country-music video programmes and to sell the single, which it most definitely did. We had line dancing and jiving on the sand, seaweed on the piano, and we finished off the evening after shooting all in one day with some well-earned beers in the Marlboro House Bar in nearby Bundoran. A very welcome treat for a very thirsty cast and crew!

The video was launched and the song's popularity continued to grow on radio and television music stations, catapulting my career on to a whole new level that was both mind-blowing and surreal. In practical terms, it meant that the dance venues we were already selling out were now too small for the crowds turning up at our gigs, and we began to look into the idea of concerts instead. I looked forward to focusing more on my vocal performance to a seated audience and offering a more sophisticated package all round. The unexpected success of 'Wagon Wheel', coupled with the years of hard work and all the reinvestment into the business, meant we could now upgrade to a bigger PA system, a bigger van and, eventually, a lorry, which is the beast you now see on the road that carries all our gear across the country all year round.

'Who is Nathan Carter?' was the question on the lips of many media personalities and, more importantly, they were asking how on earth we had managed to attract audiences from the cradle to the grave into country music, no matter where we travelled to in Ireland.

The sold-out signs were now going up in every single venue and even the country-music king of all venues, the Allingham Arms Hotel in Bundoran, was closing the doors early when word got out that we were coming to town.

Further afield, while we had already dipped our toe in the water in Scotland, it had proven to be a very different audience as, unlike Ireland, they're aren't as many regional and local radio stations to target, yet even so the strength and energy of 'Wagon Wheel' propelled us on to a new wavelength and we were able to reach out a lot more easily, as the video was picked up on different Sky channels. We teamed up with a Scottish promoter, Stewart Lawrie, who booked us into venues in Stranraer, Inverness, Aberdeen, among others, and back home we secured concerts in the theatre scene, which gave us a very different edge and allowed the younger fans to come along and enjoy our all-new show, which now focused more on the singing and the music than the dancing from before.

At one concert I recall delivering a birthday request for a three-year-old girl in the audience and for a lady who was celebrating her 101st birthday! The demographic of the people who were coming out to see us was phenomenal, and it was sometimes hard to digest just how wide and varied those audiences were becoming.

From a very small acorn, we had very gradually and very organically grown into a premium performing act that even mainstream media like BBC and RTÉ were really beginning to sit up and take notice of. It had never been simple, it was gradual and natural and a lot of hard work to get to this stage, but we were making huge waves and I now had responsibility for the livelihood not only of myself and the band members but also a crew of twelve or thirteen people who kept our show on the road.

'Wagon Wheel' spent an unbelievable forty-seven weeks on the Irish chart, and this was a year before American Billboard artist Darius Rucker had a monster hit with it also Stateside, where it went to number one for him on the Hot Country Songs chart. Incidentally, it's made a few 'banned' lists over there too, as it's just been way too popular for some people's ears, so it's not just my version, thank goodness, that has been played to the point of annoyance!

The entire reaction across the board to 'Wagon Wheel' was incredible and it continued to bounce up and down the Irish Country charts for many years – in fact, in 2017 it hit the number-one spot again, which was phenomenal.

Even fans got in on the action, with some showing their love a bit more than others, which was the case of fan and friend Ciara Devlin from Banbridge, who had a picture of the camper van tattooed on her right shoulder.

'I'd been following Nathan's shows up and down the country for a year and decided I wanted something to mark it all and, for the love of God, I couldn't think of anything until someone mentioned getting a tattoo,' says Ciara. 'I struggled to decide what I wanted to get. I'd seen that a few people had got Nathan's face and lips tattooed on various parts of their body, but I wanted something different that really represented the year we'd had, the friendships we'd made through the love of his music and the craic we'd had meeting some amazing people. So after a while thinking about it, it came to me – I'll get the camper van from the "Wagon Wheel" video! I made my way to the local tattooist and told him what I wanted, showing him stills from the video, and he looked at me like I was a bit mad . . .

'He suggested he look online himself to see if he could get a better shot of it, and I paid my deposit, booked in for a week later and, when I returned, sure enough, he had managed to find a very clear image and had it on paper – he even had the registration, so it looked exactly like the real thing! It was extremely painful and felt like he was taking lumps out of my back when he started the shading.

'I explained I wanted the words "wagon wheel" underneath it and the date and where I'd first seen Nathan perform, which was 7 July 2012 at the Mourne Country Inn in Newry and, eventually, he finished! I was absolutely amazed at what he was able to do in detail and I was in love with it at first sight. I posted it on Facebook and everyone thought I was mad. I knew Nathan would eventually see it or come across it online in some way and, sure enough, when I went to see him a fortnight later at the Mourne Country Inn again, I could see him laughing as we approached him at the meet-and-greet afterwards and he said it looked great! I still love the tattoo now as much as I did then and don't regret it one bit – and I still follow Nathan's career closely and am still having the craic and meeting more and more amazing people along the way.'

On another, less positive, note than Ciara's brave tattoo art, one fan found himself in a spot of bother over his love for the song when his neighbour got so fed up with him playing it on repeat that he broke his windows in a frustrated rage!

'I had got on fine with my neighbour, and I had been

(living) here almost a year . . . until I played Nathan Carter one night and – *boom!*' said the fan. 'I think I was playing it for an hour straight. It was an album I was playing, and it was not just "Wagon Wheel", but that is the tune that stuck in my neighbour's head.'

A court heard how the neighbour then stormed up a communal stairwell and yelled, 'If I hear "Wagon Wheel" one more time, I'm going to break that stereo!'

'Wagon Wheel', no matter how annoying or brilliant it may be 'depending on your taste' was a game-changer for me. It was a little piece of magic – the right song, the right act, the right time – I suppose you could say that, most of all, we were ready for it and the timing was absolutely perfect.

The song has brought many people great joy and many people a bit of earache (sorry!), but to me it will always be the one that will get the audience on their feet, even the most cynical man, woman or child. There's no denying it, it really captivates an audience, no matter where I bring it.

God bless you, Bob Dylan and Old Crow Medicine Show – oh, and Aisling, of course, for her wacky choice of phone ringtones in the first place, not to mention Jonathan's excellent production in the studio.

And I bet that those people who claim to hate the song secretly sing along and dance to it when no one is watching . . . they'd just never admit it.

As for me, I've so much to thank that song for, including securing me a slot on Ireland's coveted, very famous Friday-night TV programme *The Late Late Show*.

14. On the Box

Every Friday night, for a full two hours after 9.30 p.m., most households across the island of Ireland will down tools and tune into a TV chat show called *The Late Late Show*, fondly shortened and known to many as simply *The Late Late*.

'Who's on *The Late Late* tonight?' is a common question of a Friday afternoon and, as a singer or a band in Ireland, it's a big rubber stamp that you've finally made it when you're invited to perform in its famous Donnybrook studios to a broadcast audience of at least half a million people.

On top of it being somewhat of an Irish institution, *The Late Late* is also the world's second-longest-running late-night talk show, after the American *The Tonight Show* and is recognized as the official flagship television programme of Ireland's public service broadcaster *Raidió Teilifís Éireann* (RTÉ).

For two years, since the beginning of my life on the road in Ireland, we'd pitched to *The Late Late*, hoping to win a slot in front of its live studio audience. Those lucky enough to get tickets go home every week armed with goodies supplied by businesses promoting everything from fancy candles and perfumes to free flights to the UK. To date, it hadn't happened, but a chance meeting with its longest-serving presenter, Gay Byrne, would make sure that all changed.

Gay, or Uncle Gaybo, as he is fondly known, is an Irish institution himself, having been propelled into everyone's living room each Friday night for a total of thirty-seven years. He was the first broadcaster, during his days with Granada TV in England, to have introduced The Beatles on to the small screen. Although retired from the chat-show driving seat since 2009, Gay still hadn't taken his eye off the ball when I met him one night in Fermanagh after I'd performed a few songs at Father Brian D'Arcy's annual novena at the Graan Monastery, a very well-attended annual prayer service which attracted inspirational speakers from the business, media, sports, music and arts scenes.

I was invited to sing a few songs and I chose to perform the hymn 'Lady of Knock', the Scottish classic 'Caledonia' and 'Wagon Wheel', as it was hot property and very popular at the time. After the novena was over, we mingled and chatted, and Gay asked me had I ever been on *The Late Late Show*. When he heard that I hadn't, he said he'd put in a word for me.

Sure enough, true to his word, Gay played my music that Sunday on his RTÉ radio show and not long after that I got the call from Dermot McEvoy, the music supervisor of the show, that I'd waited on for so long. I was finally invited to perform on *The Late Late* but, to my surprise, they didn't want me to sing 'Wagon Wheel', thinking it wasn't well enough known just yet and, while I was surprised, as by then, a month after its release, I knew it was catching on, none of us was to know just how big it was going to be. I gave them a few other options and they chose the Green Day song 'Time of My Life', which was the title of my most recent album then. I was absolutely thrilled and so excited when the Friday afternoon came around and we drove into those studios to make our *Late Late* debut.

The show's host, Ryan Tubridy, was welcoming and charming, and we had an absolute ball, enjoying every moment of being in the famous Green Room, where drinks were served and fellow guests mingled nervously while waiting on their turn to shine.

We were all on a real high afterwards. We really felt like

we had ticked off another milestone – and we had, as this TV appearance led to a lot more recognition on the streets, in restaurants, in bars, and even one night in a urinal, when someone took a photo of me, much to my absolute horror!

Speaking of toilets, I've accidentally overheard many conversations about me on a night out or even at early gigs when we had to use the same bathrooms as the audience. Overhearing opinions of the not-so-nice variety is always very uncomfortable and embarrassing and, no matter how thick-skinned I try to be, some of the negative comments I have heard have been hurtful, even though I totally recognize that it's all part and parcel of being in the public eye. I try not to read tweets, especially after television appearances, as some of the keyboard warriors can be very ruthless, and if I do take a sneak peek I regret it afterwards, as I know I should be thinking about the hundreds of positive comments I hear instead of dwelling on those few negative ones.

Despite any of those minor incidents, being recognized is a huge compliment, of course, and 95 per cent of people who approach me have only good things to say. I love chatting to them, plus, it shows that people are interested in my music, which is always a big bonus.

The appearance on *The Late Late* definitely opened a lot of doors for me, and I've enjoyed returning many times since to Donnybrook, as both an interview guest and as a performer. Only a year later I was invited back to perform 'Wagon Wheel', which was *still* topping the charts over twelve months after it was released.

Many of those more recent *Late Late* slots were memorable – in fact, all of them are – but one in particular was truly special: when I was invited to lend my voice to a posthumous album by Mullingar legend Joe Dolan on an album called *Orchestrated* with the RTÉ orchestra.

My first photo shoot for my first album, *Starting Out*

Performing on stage in the Inishowen Gateway Hotel, Buncrana, 4 May 2009 (credit Bernadette Friel)

The silver suit!

With my cousin Savannah, Grumps, Nan, Jake, Kiara and my cousin Molly on a family night out

Nan selling merchandise

Forever friends: me and Lisa McHugh

John Sheahan from
The Dubliners and
myself backstage on
*The Nathan Carter
Show*

On stage at Holycross Festival,
Tipperary (credit Caroline
Walsh)

Myself and Terry Wogan in the BBC Radio 2 studios

With the Rose of Tralee, 2016

On tour in Australia: myself and the guys in the band

Billy Ocean and myself on stage on *The Nathan Carter Show*

Singing a duet with Mary Black on *The Nathan Carter Show*

These faces need no introduction … Enjoying a few pints after the 'Boat to Liverpool' video shoot

Dara Ó Briain and myself having the craic

I was given the hit song 'Make Me an Island' to record and, via the magic of archive footage, I was able to perform a duet with the man himself on live television. I'd never met Joe in real life, but my nan was a huge fan when she was growing up, and Joe used to come and play in Liverpool when I was about three or four years old. Nan was probably one of the women up at the front of his gigs throwing knickers at him! We had all his records and VHS tapes in the house, so when I was growing up I knew a lot of his songs and when I got the call to sing on the album it was a huge privilege. I was so honoured, and didn't realize that I was the only person on the album to actually get to do a duet with the man himself. His vocal range is extraordinary – he can sing so high. I'm quite a high singer myself, but when I heard the key of the song I had to have it lowered to meet those big notes.

Another iconic moment for me on *The Late Late Show* was the chance to duet with a fellow Liverpudlian – the truly legendary Charlie Landsborough, who always has been a hero of mine. Charlie and I had recorded a version of his huge hit 'Forever Friend' in 2011 in Nashville for my *Time of My Life* album, and to perform it with him on Ireland's biggest weekly chat show was a moment that filled me with great pleasure. We also sang 'Boat to Liverpool', a song I'd written which leads into the, for me, very nostalgic sounds of 'Leaving of Liverpool', and when Charlie joined me on stage for that part of the song my heart swelled with pride.

To be invited on to *The Late Late Show*, no matter how many times it has happened down the years now, is always something I will never take for granted. It shows a massive leap forward for country music in Ireland. It's not typical, perhaps, of a city audience to understand the popularity of the country-dance culture in rural towns and cities, so for

RTÉ to recognize and acknowledge that market is a pat on the shoulder for us in the business. This faith in viewers' choice was further recognized with the recording of a *Late Late Show Country Special* which featured a host of stars, including legends such as Daniel O'Donnell, Margo, Philomena Begley, Foster and Allen, Brian Coll, Susan McCann and Big Tom, as well as lots of us newer faces, like Cliona, Derek Ryan, Lisa McHugh, Johnny Brady and many more. The atmosphere on the night of that recording was one of respect and friendship, and the fact that so many artists started playing country music some fifty years ago and are still doing it now proves the longevity of the love there is out there for it.

Everyone was very down to earth and we all got together at the end of the show to perform a rendition of 'Country Roads', which was great fun. We partied afterwards at Lillie's Bordello nightclub, where I recall enjoying the most expensive vodka I've ever tasted in my life with Jimmy Buckley and Aidan Quinn!

I totally adore a good old catch-up with all those guys, especially the likes of Daniel O'Donnell, and nights like the *Late Late Show Country Special* give a great opportunity for a chat and a bit of a laugh. Daniel has been very good to me down the years and is never afraid to lend an ear or to give me a bit of advice when it comes to breaking new territories. He's been part of my family musically for as long as I can remember and is always at the end of the phone if I ever need him. I've also enjoyed being part of the bill with him on TG4's *Opry an Lúir.*

One of perhaps my most memorable moments on television came about on the night of the country special when I was sharing the sofa with Philomena Begley. The media had a field day when I made an innuendo-filled blunder and my face went bright pink with embarrassment.

Referring to the night in Donegal when Philomena had invited me up on stage all those years ago, and referring to my 'rise to fame' since then, I said:

'To be honest, I wouldn't be sitting here only for Philomena. Philomena was the first woman ever in Ireland to get me up.'

The audience erupted and, realizing my gaffe, I put my head in my hands and said, 'Oh Jesus,' as Philomena laughed her head off in response.

I suppose you could say that nerves got the better of me and I totally walked into that one but, as the saying goes, there's no such thing as bad publicity, and the video clip subsequently went viral.

Even after so many appearances on television, I still do get nervous and I've never been comfortable with being on camera. I'm even more nervous for television, especially if it's live, than I am for my own live gigs, as it's very much out of my comfort zone and I'd much rather be singing than talking. I'm mostly afraid of falling over, forgetting the words or what I am going to say or being overcome with anxiety and just freezing on the spot.

Nerves have often caught me unawares and perhaps another of the more stand-out times was when we were playing a dance at the Four Seasons Hotel in Monaghan back in the early days. As always, I had to use the loo before the show. I knew that we had to be onstage at 10.30 p.m., but when I came out of the bathroom there was no one to be seen. The band had already gone on stage and I could hear them in the distance playing the intro which was to mark my big arrival to join them. At this particular venue, the access to the stage was through the kitchen but, when I got there, the door was locked and I could see the boys onstage through the window, I could hear them, but they couldn't hear me, despite me banging on the glass. I ended up running outside, around the side of the hotel, and passed through the foyer of the main entrance, where punters were queuing up to get in. By the time I made it through the dance hall I had to wait at the side of the stage, as the band had given up waiting on me and the bass player Jimmy had decided to sing a song so I had to wait until he was finished!

Before I go on live TV my nerves really do hit a peak, so to help me manage any anxiety before it kicks in I tend to sing as loudly as I can into a towel to try and release some of the stress. It works to an extent, but when the cameras start rolling I can always feel myself break out in a light sweat and I just have to hope for the best.

Being on television brings many fantastic opportunities, of course, and I've also been a guest on the *Imelda May Show*, where I performed with Imelda, Sharon Shannon and Finbar Furey, three artists who I really admire, and the BBC's *Nolan Show*, which always attracts a big audience as well. On it I performed some songs and took part in a light-hearted panel discussions where I learned all about social etiquette, much to fellow guest Father Brian D'Arcy's amusement.

One of the biggest TV shows was the nightly magazine programme *The One Show* on BBC1, which goes out across the UK. Hosts Matt Baker and Alex Jones were filming in Ballycastle, County Antrim, as part of a feature called the Big Causeway Crawl and I was invited, along with my band, to perform 'Summer's Here', as well as have a chat on the sofa. I was joined there by none other than my nan herself, who was delighted that so many people were offering us tea all the time and that we even had our own security! The performance did attract a few new fans from the UK who may not have heard of me before, and *OK!* magazine ran a most amusing feature saying that viewers were left 'swooning', quoting one tweeter who said, 'I think Nathan Carter might be my new guilty pleasure!'

A huge step out of my comfort zone was a cameo role on TG4's Irish soap opera *Ros na Rún*. It was the first time I'd ever acted – even though I was only playing myself in the part! The show is recorded *as Gaeilge*, so I had to learn my lines in Irish. Thanks to the assistance of John Farry's sisters Patricia McPartland and Marie McShane, who are both Irish teachers and taught me the pronunciation phonetically, I eventually got a hold of it. The storyline was about a fan coming to see me in a bar and, although it's hardly Oscar-winning material or a Hollywood challenge, it was a big step for me and another thing to tell the grandchildren!

Sticking with Irish-speaking programmes, one of the best launching pads for up-and-coming singers in the business comes via another TG4 programme called *Glór Tíre*. In it, a young singer is mentored by a more well-known artist in a bid to win a six-week-long talent competition that can certainly open doors. I was delighted to have been involved twice on the show; firstly, when I was mentor to County Fermanagh's Sean Corrigan and secondly, the following year, with County Derry's Niamh McGlinchey, who I recorded a duet called 'Bruises' with. Both are very talented singers and musicians, and I still keep in touch with them and like to help them out whenever I can.

It's important for me now to try and pave the way for newcomers, as I really appreciated it when it came to my turn, and I like to tell them, just as I was told, about the real-ities of life on the road. A fantastic opportunity to show this to a wider audience came along when I was invited to take part in the popular TV3 show *Living with Lucy*, in which pre-senter Lucy Kennedy effectively moves in with a series of celebrities in a bid to show what their lives are like away from the cameras and bright lights of what they do for a living.

Lucy spent a night with her camera crew at my parents' home in Liverpool, where we wandered down memory lane, talking about my life before Ireland, and then two nights with my band and me on a trip on the tour bus to a gig in Inverness. Sharing a bus with twelve men (and Nan!) as well as a camera crew was probably more of a challenge to Lucy than it was for me, as I'm so used to the confined space and living in each other's pockets now, but she did really well, was great fun to be around and we showed her a late night on the tiles in true Nathan Carter band style! Lucy was brilliant craic and up for the laugh. Overall, it was much easier than a live TV environment, but I'll still cringe when it comes to watching it back, just like I always do!

Being in the public eye certainly brings all sorts of exciting opportunities and challenges, but at the end of the day, as far as I'm concerned, it always has to come back to creating the best music I can and coming up with the best songs I can. 'Wagon Wheel' was groundbreaking for my career, but the reality remained that I couldn't hang on to its success for ever, so it was back to the drawing board and to carefully selecting, and writing, a variety of songs that would keep my growing audience interested and wanting to hear more.

15. 'This Song is for You'

Over the next few years, following the phenomenon that was 'Wagon Wheel', for which we also recorded a live DVD of the same title, I went on to release four more albums – *Where I Wanna Be* (2013), *Beautiful Life* (2014), *Stayin' Up All Night* (2015) and *Livin' the Dream* (2016), as well as several live albums, all to great success.

As well as selecting covers to include in those albums, I was moving more into participating and contributing to writing original songs that suited both my vocals and the style of music. I wanted to record songs that were very radio-friendly and perhaps even a bit more modern than what I had done in the past.

The release of *Beautiful Life*, in 2014, which was a selection of new recordings of 'greatest hits' to date of sorts, saw a move to one of the UK's most recognized record labels, Decca Records, in a three quarter of a million pound deal that I truly thought would change my life. Soon, I found myself far from Fermanagh and rural Ireland, in boardrooms in London with approximately thirty people who all had a say in supporting my career, from publicists to music executives, from marketing experts to promoters. There was a job and a person doing it for every element of the business, and it looked like my career was about to soar to even dizzier heights.

It was exciting, it was new and, just like it would be to many artists in my position, it was a dream come true.

By this point I'd already had two number-one albums in

Ireland, and Decca were able to promise the sun, the moon and the stars, with big budgets for things we could never have thought of before. I was sent out around the UK, for example, in my own 'record-shop van', and we set up pop-up shops in city centres, shopping centres, Irish centres and schools, and by doing this we managed to push the album *Beautiful Life* into the UK Top Twenty.

As I was shipped around by this huge team of supporters, I thought back to the days in the north-west of England, and to Nan and I driving around in her little Honda Civic with hardly enough room for us to sit up straight, so packed was the car with her collection of CDs and early merchandise. Now, here I was, under the care of the big guns and with a record in the mainstream charts. It was the stuff that dreams were made of – but yet, somehow, something just didn't feel right.

Decca are amazing at what they do, there is no doubt about that, and when my second album with them, *Stayin' Up All Night*, was released, again it was a big hit, reaching number one in Ireland and sneaking into the UK Top Twenty again. The title came to me as a nod to my tendency to let my hair down after gigs when the job is done, and it was a line from my song, co-written with Don Mescall, 'Livin' the Dream'. I am generally up to the early hours of the morning – basically, to reward myself for working hard, I like to play hard too – but I was always one to make sure my feet were firmly kept on the ground. Back in Liverpool, Grumps had something to say about the title of the album.

'It's like something you'd hear in an ad for Viagra,' he told me, and I had to admit he had a point. I never thought of the title in the same way since that! Good old Grumps, making sure I didn't get carried away with it all!

Although I did learn a lot and had great success with

Decca, the genre of music that I played was not mainstream country, nor was it mainstream folk – it was Country and Irish and, eventually, we both admitted that perhaps it wasn't that easy for bigger record labels, who had no one really to compare me to, to understand, and I found it hard to explain, as my audience was as unique as the genre I was playing in. We appealed to four-year-olds, to forty-year-olds, to eighty-four year olds . . . and although that is absolutely perfect for me, it's not very straightforward for some to understand or to brand and in the end we parted ways and I went back to being independently published, just as I was before, and to be honest, it's just how I like it.

Within eighteen months of leaving Decca, I had all the publishing rights back and, with that, comes the responsibility again, and the freedom of having control over everything from singles, albums, venues, tours to all that we had managed to date so well before.

And in between all that, I kept on writing songs . . .

The idea for a song, be it a line of catchy lyrics, a melody, a chorus or even just a title, can come to me at the rarest of times, so I always jot down notes on to my phone or record myself humming a tune if the muse strikes when I'm on the move. Many, many times I've woken up in the middle of the night with a cracking concept, promising myself that I'll remember it in the morning, but I wake up again in daylight having totally lost what I had come up with, and that is so frustrating, but all too common for many songwriters, or so I hear.

I consider myself very much a performer, firstly. My voice and musicality are where my strengths lie, and I hold people who can churn out a song easily in the greatest respect but, for me, songwriting doesn't always come naturally. What does come naturally is the ability to sing it when it's all done, but sometimes it takes a while to get to that stage if I'm to work on songwriting alone.

The idea of co-writing is a very popular way of songwriting in Nashville, and it's something that is really taking off here in Ireland and the UK now. Rarely will an artist work alone without a second party coming on board to lend some expertise, whether it's in the lyric or the melody, and I'm blessed to have worked with many great songwriters down the years who have either written fantastic songs to suit my vocal range, or worked with me on ideas I have to bring them to life.

My manager, John Farry, had already had songwriting success, of course, when I met him, so I have enjoyed many a session with him on guitar while I brainstorm on the keyboards and, suddenly, it all comes together. I also enjoy writing with Joe McShane, who is a brother of Nicky James, and I've also worked with Ralph Murphy in Nashville, who is a British-born Canadian songwriter who has written for Shania Twain, Randy Travis and Cliff Richard, to name a few. More recently, I've been honoured to spend many very productive writing sessions with Don Mescall, a Limerick man now based in London.

Everyone I know has a different approach to what makes a good song. For example, the song 'Christmas Stuff' from my album of the same name was born out of a title, when Ralph (Murphy) came into the room to me and John Farry and just blurted it out. It was all he had so far, so I began to tinkle a few notes on the keyboard and soon we had a melody, then the lyrics came and, between the three of us, the song was born.

'Temple Bar' does exactly what it says on the tin. I'd been going there on nights out at every opportunity when visiting Dublin since I was about twenty-two years old, and I often joke onstage when introducing the song that it's the type of place you remember going to but rarely remember coming out of! I absolutely love it there, and I don't think I've ever been on a street like it, where there are so many cultures and nationalities, all absorbing the unique atmosphere or street entertainment and music that leaks out of every bar. I tried to capture this atmosphere in the song, mentioning the buskers on every corner, the 'people there from everywhere to God knows where' and the infectious feel-good factor that you can get only there. The song was created one afternoon at my house in Enniskillen when John and I were writing together, and I do believe that, in the same session, we came up with 'Skinny Dippin''', an attempt – pardon the pun – to dip my toe in the water of something a little bit risqué. I've always loved to perform the Joe Nicholl's song 'Tequila Makes Her Clothes Fall Off', and I was aiming for something along those lines, so the idea of skinny-dipping came to mind. I looked up the title and couldn't believe that it hadn't been used, and we got to work. Sure enough, the risqué element soon caught on, and it's during that song on tour that I get all sorts of ladies' underwear thrown up on to the stage. We even have a drawer now dedicated to all the variety of colours, shapes and sizes – in fact, some of it seems to disappear sometimes. Maybe someone is treating their lady friend on the cheap when they spot an item that takes their fancy!

'Goodtime Girls' is an up-tempo sing-along song that was pitched to me by an Irish writer called P. J. Murrihy, who had come across a song recorded by Bruce Springsteen called 'Buffalo Girls' that used an old nursery-rhyme-type melody from old-time America. Bruce had made up his own lyrics to the very memorable melody, so between myself and John we came up with our own version and it has become a firm favourite at all our gigs over the past four years.

When it comes to penning tracks from the heart, one of the main songs from my collection that comes to mind is one entitled simply 'Liverpool'. I wrote it along with Joe McShane, and it's definitely up there with my favourites, as it means so much to me, being all about the place I was born in and grew up in, with so many precious memories of my childhood. I wanted to recognize the music of Liverpool, the Beatles, John and Paul, among others, and it also touches on the Hillsborough disaster of 1989 when ninety-six people were killed during the FA Cup semifinal at Hillsborough Stadium. I know many people who lost someone that day, so it's my very small way of remembering their loved ones, and I take great pride in the words every time I get the chance to perform it. Despite living in Ireland and loving it so much for the past eight years, there is always a piece of my heart at home, and I have had many people shake my hand, even those who don't particularly follow or even like my genre of music, and tell me that the song hits a chord with them and, to me, that's the best compliment I can ever receive. I love Liverpool – the culture, the music – everything about it; it's a great city and I think that Liverpool people are the most genuine, the most caring and the most good-hearted, plus, their sense of humour is second to none. I often think of the shops, the Irish Centre, the Liffey Bar and the people I used to meet there, and I miss it sometimes. I miss it a lot.

I'm lucky to be able to touch people with my music and I never take that for granted, nor do I take for granted the people who have followed me down the years, so I wrote a song called 'Thank You', which is my way of reaching out to the fan base who have been so loyal to me from the start. My fans are very happy people – very lively, let's say – and I wanted to sing a song to them to show how much I appreciate all their support through thick and thin, to those who travelled and continue to do so, to those who buy the CDs, the tickets, everything, so I wrote this song with them in mind.

It's a very personal song to me and I hope they like it as much as I enjoy singing it to them.

16. Love, Fans and Friendship

The price of fame – or life on the road, at least – is the difficulty in maintaining and sustaining long-term friendships and relationships outside of your band and the fans and faces that you see along the way.

I like to be approachable when it comes to fans, and I chat and mingle at meet-and-greets after my shows for as long as I can, which means that I do get to know not only faces, but names and the life stories of those who follow me and travel around the country to hear my music, which is a nice thing to be able to do for as long as I can keep it up.

I take my relationship with my fans very seriously and communicate with them in every way possible, especially through social media, which I try to update daily when I can. I also have a very reliable and trustworthy friend, Denise Frazer, who looks after the modern-day equivalent of a fan club. Denise and I meet once a month and decide on news output, which she then compiles into a newsletter and emails it out to an established database, plus, I take the time to sign cards and read letters that have come to her for my attention, always doing my best to send a personal response as far as I possibly can.

Another family I have become close to are three generations of the Nolan family – Leanne, Pamela and Evelyn – who have been with me from the very first gig in Ireland. Leanne now runs my website and the Nathan Carter app which tells fans dates of gigs, news and other exclusive stuff that can only be found out when you sign up to it. I'm delighted now to be able to call these people who work closely with me my friends, and I really appreciate everything they do.

Some of the fans are very creative and, as well as tattoos, one young lady, twelve-year-old Cara Cronly, caught my eye online recently when she had a 'Nathan and Jake' manicure in preparation for my concert, with tiny pictures of me and my brother on her fingernails. The story of this even made the pages of *VIP* magazine, which was pretty impressive.

I think, no matter what business you work in, and no matter how many people there are in your life to turn to, there can never be enough, and I know that I have many people to call very good friends. One of the people I have come to know and trust is Father Brian D'Arcy. I know I can talk to him about anything. As well as being there for me on a personal level, Father Brian is a great sounding board for new songs or ideas, and I know he has helped a lot of people in the country-music business by listening and giving out some good advice when it's asked for.

There's great camaraderie in the country-music scene – a bit of rivalry too, I'm sure – but I do have some fun people who I love to hang out with when the opportunity arises and who I keep in touch with on a regular basis, such as Cliona Hagan, Niamh McGlinchey and Johnny Brady. We regularly Snapchat and meet up with each other when we can – as far as our hectic schedules allow for, these days!

Outside of the music business, unfortunately, but I suppose inevitably, I've definitely drifted away from many of those people from my schooldays, but I often think of them and what they are up to now, plus, I do love to bump into an old familiar face if the opportunity ever arises. I left school at a very young age, when my peers were entering their A-level years and then going on to study at university, so our paths took us in very different directions and I sometimes do wish that I could have stayed in touch more with them. However, I also believe that, in life, we meet new people along the way who can still be your closest friends even if you haven't known them for ever, and I'm very lucky to have a solid group of friends in Enniskillen, where I've lived since I left Ann and Jim's house in Donegal about seven years ago.

In the past six years I've grown very close to my own tribe, who I can call on day or night, and that's Cathal, his sisters Aisling and Kerri, our good friend Bronagh, my drummer Gareth and his fiancée, Emma, and of course Lisa (McHugh), who all live nearby. We meet up as often as we can, we go on holidays together and, one night when we were out in Enniskillen, Gareth popped the question – he asked me to be godfather to his new baby daughter, Abbie. To say I was emotional is an understatement! I was absolutely over the moon; in fact, I think it was probably the nicest thing anyone has ever said to me and I now take my godfather duties very seriously, making sure my now little two-year-old buddy has a friend in me. After she was born we had a big christening party for her at the Bush in Enniskillen and the band All Folk'd Up played at it, so we really marked her grand arrival in style. Abbie is a bubbly, adorable little girl, and one of my favourite pastimes now is looking after her as often as I can – she really is a bundle of joy, and she has really taken to my brother, Jake, who is now part of the gang also, since he moved to Fermanagh to live with me.

I've also been asked to do the honour of being Gareth's best man at his wedding to Emma in the winter of 2018, which is a role I am also taking very seriously, especially when it comes to arranging a stag party in Las Vegas for a very eager group of men from Tyrone and Fermanagh who are chomping at the bit to sample life in one of the world's most renowned party cities. Hopefully, we will all make it back in one piece! I think I'm looking forward to it and dreading it a bit at the same time, but it will be all good, clean, healthy fun I'm sure. Won't it, lads?

I know it's not easy finding a home from home when you're an English man in a different country, but I feel a very strong connection to the people of Ireland, maybe due to my own Irish roots and my Nan's Northern background, but also because of the characteristics that Irish people and Liverpudlians share – humour, loyalty, maybe, and definitely a love of music and being up for the craic.

Enniskillen in County Fermanagh has become that home from home for me, and I'm very much in love with the place. It's a border town that suits me and my interests so well, as it's on the beautiful Lough Erne, an island town that lends itself to rural living, with its picturesque surroundings, as well as having all the amenities of a big town on your doorstep. I'm a boating fanatic and have great memories of going out on my uncle's speedboat as a child – I learned to jet-ski off the back of it when I was just eight years old – so to live so close to the water is ideal for me, and I couldn't ask for anything better. I was instantly hooked at that young age by the rush of adrenaline, the speed of the boat, the splash of the waves and the carefree feeling that being out on the wide-open space of the water brings. It's an ideal way to unwind, especially for someone like me who finds it so hard to switch off. I do believe that there's some sort of a therapy in being out on a boat. Maybe it's the isolation and the feeling of getting away from it all but, whatever it is, it works for me, and it's my favourite way to spend time with my friends, so much so that I'm now on my third boat and, only last year, my dad, Jake and I got our powerboat licence, which comes in handy when we want to show some friends a day out with a difference.

As well as a passion for boats, I also have a great love of cars and my bedroom walls as a child always had a glossy poster of a fast car like a Ferrari or a Jaguar on them. I'd dream of one day owning or at least getting a spin in one of them, if I was lucky. At my last count I've gone through fourteen vehicles in nine years, including my first little Renault Kangoo van, and I'm known to be really bad at holding on to cars, always deciding to change them when the novelty wears off. I bought an Aston Martin DBS in 2007, and it was my dream car, but even so I only kept it for six months as I just felt guilty for owning it and the attention that came with it. It was a petrol model and it was amazing, but oh so loud, and I couldn't have driven it down the street without drawing a lot of interest my way, so I decided that it was too flash, plus, I was afraid of someone scratching it – and who needs stress like that! I'd rather enjoy a car than live with that type of worry, so I said goodbye to the Aston Martin. But it was fun while it lasted!

I'm often asked in interviews what I'd like in my ideal woman, and I joke that she would have to be into cars like I am! I don't know mechanically how they work (cars, I mean, not women!), but I do know a lot about engine sizes, the look of them and I've watched every episode of *Top Gear* and *Fifth Gear* that have ever been broadcast.

Back to my ideal woman, though . . . I don't have a particular type at all, but I do like someone who shares a similar sense of humour and I'd really love to find someone that can make me laugh a lot. I hold my parents' marriage and their relationship in very high regard – they are the epitome of what's known in modern-day lingo as 'relationship goals', but I know, realistically, that it may not be as easy for me to find what they have, no matter how much I'd love it to happen.

Life on the road means a lot of trust, especially if one

partner isn't in the music business, and trust is a big thing for me when in a relationship. I find it probably a bit too easy to trust people and I'm often told that it's my downfall by my close friends and family, who know me best. I'm a private person living in the public eye, so anyone I have in my close circle, be it romantically or as a friend, has to know that trust is way up there on my list, and I'll reward their trust in return, but I know that real life isn't always as simple as that.

I do enjoy female company and I've been told I'm quite flirtatious when I like someone, though I never notice that myself – I'm definitely not a typical ladies' man, but when I like someone, I like someone and I wouldn't be afraid to show it. I love going to the cinema to see action movies and doing all the usual 'night in' stuff like watching Netflix with a Chinese takeaway and a tub of Häagen-Dazs ice cream and, of course, it would be lovely to have someone to share that with when I come home from a few days, weeks, or even months on the road.

In saying that, at twenty-eight years old, I don't feel any pressure at all right now, nor am I in a rush to meet 'the one'.

People of my generation don't get married as young as my parents did, so I feel like I've plenty of time and, believe me, I'm enjoying every moment of these single years when I can focus on my career, travel the world and meet lots and lots of people from all walks of life.

Who knows, someday I might have a nice big home on the water in Fermanagh, a holiday home in the sun, a few mini-Carters running around my feet, and I'll be barking at them not to touch the shiny collection of Aston Martins in the garage as my lady waves me off to sing my songs and play my music.

You never know, it might happen one day. Watch this space!

17. Giving Something Back

My parents and grandparents instilled in me from a very young age that it was always important to give something back whenever you can, be it to a charity, to someone who needs a helping hand or to those who are worse off in life, and I try to live by those morals as best I can. I think it probably stems from Nan feeling a little bit guilty when I was making money from singing at such a young age. Even when I wasn't meant to be given money people would hand me some, and she always made me put some of it aside to support a local charity or cause.

Grumps had a pot in the house that he made me put any spare change I had into, and I always felt better for it, just like he said I would, and again, that has stuck with me. I did a lot of gigs in my teens to help raise money to send sick children my age and younger to Lourdes, and I also went to Lourdes myself to help out when I was about ten or eleven. It was a very rewarding and truly educational experience to see other children who couldn't do a lot of the things that we often take for granted. Many of them were wheelchair bound, some of them were terminally ill, but they taught me a lot, including how to show gratitude, strength and resilience, and I will never forget it.

It's impossible, of course, to be able to fulfil every charitable request that comes my way nowadays, as there are so, so many, but I do my best to reach out and give something back when I can to those who need it or to people who touch my heart with their story.

A phone call to someone who isn't feeling well, a card to someone who is sick in hospital, a shout-out from the stage or a mention on the radio is the least I can do to show my appreciation to all the people who continue to support me in my career through thick and thin.

I'm in a privileged position, whereby I get to meet and play to thousands of people across the world every year, and many of my fans have learning and intellectual difficulties as well as other disabilities, so I'm honoured that my music is a source of joy for them.

I first met little Padraig McErlean from Castledawson back in 2012 when he was just two years old. Padraig, who has Down's syndrome, is a big fan of the song 'Wagon Wheel', and when I saw his very own rendition on Facebook just this year it really tugged at my heart strings. Everyone was liking and sharing the video, trying to make sure I would see it, so I decided to record a reply to Padraig, and I invited him and his parents to come along to my next arena gig in Belfast.

'Padraig has loved Nathan's music since a charity night we did back with him in 2012,' says Padraig's dad, Donard. 'Ever since then there seems to be a connection with Nathan, and he just loves when "Wagon Wheel" comes on. He just sings and sings and it makes him happy. When he saw the video he could not believe Nathan Carter knew his name! He watches it on the iPad and loves it!'

Padraig is a real charmer and I always love to bump into him and his parents. He's growing up to be quite a singer too, so I'd better watch myself, as I could have some stiff competition just around the corner if his videos keep going viral!

I try not to let fans down, especially when they have travelled so far to come and see me, so I was faced with quite a conundrum when, due to Storm Ophelia, we had to cancel a recent concert at Cork Opera House. I knew that there were lots of disappointed fans staying in our hotel, which just happened to have a lovely piano in the bar, so I decided that, if we couldn't make it to the opera house, then we'd bring the opera house to us, and I sat down at the piano and sang a few songs, much to everyone's surprise. The fact that there was no electricity added to the atmosphere, and it was certainly a performance with a difference, but it was worth it just to see the smiling faces of people who otherwise would have been stuck in their hotel room without even a light to switch on. It's always good to think outside of the box, and it was a moment that we all will remember fondly, singing at the top of our voices as the wind and rain battered against the windows.

That same week I was meant to visit the Marymount Hospice in Cork, which offers specialist palliative care to patients both onsite and out in the community. One local businessman, George O'Dwyer from the Hazel Tree venue in Mallow, gave me my first chance in County Cork when I was starting out, and I have never forgotten it, so when George asked me to help raise some funds for the hospice I didn't even pause for thought. While the visit was stalled by Storm Ophelia, we did go ahead on a later date with a fundraising concert with the aim of raising €15–20,000 through ticket sales and raffle prizes. On the day of the concert I was given the heartiest of welcomes by the Lord Mayor of Cork, Tony Fitzgerald, who introduced me to his staff and showed me round the council offices, and when we played the gig, we were gobsmacked when we heard that it had in fact raised a grand total of €50,000, which will go a long way towards helping the hospice to keep on providing its current level of much-needed services.

One of the worthiest charities I have ever worked for is

the Irish charity Make a Wish, which gives terminally ill children the chance to live out a life-changing dream – anything from meeting their favourite singer or actor or sports star to swimming with dolphins or holidaying in Disneyland.

It was truly an honour when I was contacted by the charity to help grant the wish of a little eleven-year-old girl called Katie Cronin who is battling Hodgkin's lymphoma and who wanted to meet me in advance of my upcoming concert in Leopardstown.

We celebrated Katie's birthday with a guitar-shaped cake and I signed her own guitar. Katie, who is from Cork, is herself a talented musician and she happily picked up her guitar and sang 'Wagon Wheel' with me. I was blown away by her performance. To make her day as memorable as it could possibly be, I then invited her to help me present the trophy to the winners of the Nathan Carter Handicap Race at Leopardstown Racecourse before I took to the stage. I hope that Katie is still singing – what a strong and brave little girl she proved to be that day.

It was also a true privilege to raise funds for the Red Cross at the Inishowen Flood Aid Concert in Letterkenny, along with a host of performers, including Daniel O'Donnell, Dominic Kirwan, Barry Kirwan and many more, who lent their time for such a great cause. The event was to try and help the many families and individuals who have been devastatingly affected by the severe flooding in that area at the time.

In the west of Ireland one night I was keeping a low profile in the lobby of my Ennis hotel before my gig while the Clare Division Older Persons Christmas party was in full swing in the function room when a member of the gardaí noticed me and asked if I would bring my guitar into the Christmas party.

How could I say no? So I grabbed a guitar and strummed

my way into the party, singing 'Wagon Wheel', and within a minute more than half of the party were up on their feet dancing!

The gardaí thanked me and, by the time we'd all had selfies taken with the guests, it took a while to get out of the room. It was great fun!

In County Louth we do an annual fundraiser for the Maria Goretti Foundation's Children's Respite Centre in Lordship. A very good friend of the band, Peter Hanlon, is one of the team involved in the foundation, which offers respite care in the picturesque Cooley mountains for children aged six to eighteen years with disabilities and life-limiting conditions. For the past three years we've helped to raise much-needed funds which go towards the amazing facilities at the centre, and it's a joy to see the smiling faces of the children as they sing and dance along to the music during our show.

At a more local level, I like to support County Fermanagh charities and causes as much as I possibly can, and I was delighted to go along to Willowbank Special School to sign autographs and sing a few songs in aid of their minibus appeal. The pupils at the school tend to learn a lot out in the community, plus, they needed a vehicle to take them to appointments with the doctor or dentist, to go shopping or to the hairdresser's. The event was organized by the local Rotary Club and it was great fun to hang out with all the pupils, their teachers and carers and, again, some of the singers could give me a run for my money!

Every Christmas in Fermanagh there's a fundraising grotto and I show my face in there as often as I can. Also, I like to get my hands dirty when the opportunity arises so I got stuck in recently in aid of Cancer Connect when they were building a new water-sports centre near where I live. I helped brush up, clean up and dropped people off when they needed lifts. Those days on the building site with my dad weren't in vain after all, as my learned labouring skills definitely came in handy.

I love Christmas and have many fond memories of growing up in a very loving family with my grandparents and parents making a fuss, so it's always a time when I try and think of those who are going through difficult times. I enjoy dropping off selection boxes to the children's ward at the local hospital for the little ones who won't get home for Santa coming. It really is a time of year that makes me think of how it must feel to be up against illness and other challenges, especially when the rest of us are celebrating and enjoying the festivities, so I just slip in and leave them off some chocolate treats, which hopefully puts a smile on their wee faces.

It's so heartbreaking to hear of a child being sick and I dread to think of what some families have to go through, so I was so honoured to meet the parents of an eight-year-old girl called Ellie Nicholl who in 2016 lost her fight to a rare neurological condition called H-ABC syndrome, which affects just one in 318 million people. Ellie's brave parents, Billy and Ciara, distraught at the loss of such a young, beautiful child, now offer free respite breaks to families who have also suffered such loss in a pretty corner of County Fermanagh where they can have anonymity, space and spend time in a very cosy and comfortable static mobile home tucked away from real life and give themselves a chance to reflect and breathe and, hopefully, find some comfort. I was truly honoured when Billy and Ciara invited me to be the official ambassador for the project, which allows me to help promote it in any way I can. The bravery and generosity of some people really does blow me away, and they have truly made Ellie's Retreat a place that is fit for a princess, just like their little girl, who gained her angel wings far too soon.

Hearing about such heartache, loss and sadness stays with you, and I am always reminding myself how much of an honour it is to be asked to support charities and individuals going through tough times.

Perhaps the most touching moments are those spent with fans who are preparing to leave this life and, although it kills me inside, I try and go with their family's wishes as far as I can when I get a call to visit someone who is facing their end of days.

It's a very heart-tugging, soul-searching and highly emotional experience, especially knowing that your song or voice is one of the last things that they may have requested before leaving this world. It always breaks my heart to do so, but it puts everything into perspective and it humbles me greatly to know that I can give just a few moments of happiness to them in the very saddest of times.

I always walk away with a lump in my throat but a glow in my heart that I have done my best to try and make those people happy, even if it's just for some precious minutes which they and their loved ones can cling on to as the inevitable day comes around.

I suppose that's the journey I'm on, and I have to keep going, not knowing sometimes where I'm going to end up next or the situations I'm going to share with so many special people.

In this very privileged work that I do, I just never know where it's going to take me next. I know now what it can be to experience moments of the deepest despair, the lowest of lows or the highest of highs, and it takes me to many new places I never thought I'd see.

I know being a singer and entertainer is in my blood and that it comes naturally to me, despite how nervous I still become before stepping out on stage, whether it's in Donegal or Detroit or Doncaster – so when a company called Tyrone Productions approached me with a whole new challenge that meant me facing one of my biggest fears – speaking on TV – it was something I had to think really carefully about. Could I overcome any fear of stuttering, stammering, falling or putting my foot in it for not one, not two, not even three but six shows, where I would not only be the musical entertainment but also the main host?

I thought about it for ... well, for about five minutes, before I said yes, and told myself I'd get over any doubts in my mind as to whether or not I could do it. The programme was to be a Christmas special for RTÉ, home of *The Late Late Show*, and it's not something I could ever have turned down, now is it?

Yes, every day is a school day in this business, and I was just about to learn one of my greatest lessons to date – how to be a TV host on my very own *Nathan Carter Show*.

18. *The Nathan Carter Show*

The idea for the Christmas special TV show was that it should be a kind of chat show with live performances by guest singers and bands, interspersed by songs from myself and some chat with the audience and, the more I thought about it, although it really was going to mean stepping out of my comfort zone, I found it to be a great idea and an excellent career move, due to the exposure it would bring and the challenge it would throw me into – not to mention the excitement over who my special guests might be.

Tyrone Productions is one of Ireland's largest and highly renowned television production companies and has a strong national and international presence. Their work, which has been established over the past thirty years, includes well-known programmes that cover many genres – factual, entertainment, drama, documentary, live events and children's output – and include *The All Ireland Talent Show*, *Ros na Rún*, *School around the Corner*, *Wanderlust* and the legendary *Riverdance*.

I met up with producer Patricia Moore and I knew instantly that I was in good hands. We talked through ideas for the show's format, about potential guests, filming locations (going with Mansion House in Dublin for the Christmas special), and I was coached on how to deliver a script, how to interview celebrities and even how to stand when in front of the camera. It was quite an education and I thoroughly enjoyed learning more and more of what it took to present a show and perform and sing on it as well.

Singing, I quickly discovered, was the easy part. Presenting and interviewing was a different beast altogether and, at the beginning, I was told that I was speaking way too fast and needed to slow down. I was given questions to ask each guest and I wasn't allowed to use cue cards or an autocue – it would come across as less contrived and more natural that way – but, to be honest, this just made me more nervous and I had to really focus on what to say to each of the very talented people who I had the honour of chatting to.

The audience was made up of invited guests, including a lot of my family from Liverpool, and this did help me cope with my nerves a bit better when it came to the actual recording. The live audience created a magical atmosphere and gave me some focus but, looking back, it may have been better if I'd just come up with my own questions and gone a bit more with the flow, but, that said, it was a pilot programme and we all were learning.

The guests were a treat to work with – we had Irish singing legend Mary Black, who talked about her magnificent career which spans over forty years. Singer-songwriter Paddy Casey from Dublin was a pleasure to chat to, The Dubliners' John Sheahan was also on the bill, The Shires popped in to perform their latest single and the Dublin Gospel Choir lent a lovely Christmas feel to the programme, which was topped off with a truly festive performance of 'The Rare Auld Times' by myself, Mary, Paddy and John.

The show went out in December 2015 and I couldn't believe it when the ratings came in – almost 600,000 people had watched it! Both RTÉ and Tyrone Productions, not to mention me and the band, were all delighted, and I felt like I had achieved something brand new. For me, it was a lot more intense than doing a gig. There was a lot more to take on board – trying to look as energetic as possible, remembering the interview questions for the guests, worrying about the music and singing the songs. But when I saw the finished article, I was relieved to see that it looked great.

Tyrone Productions were blown away by demand for audience tickets. They only put out the audience call for the show about two weeks in advance and they had over nine hundred email requests to come within less than twenty-four hours. I think it went up at about 10 p.m on my website and, by the following morning, their inbox was full to bursting. From those nine hundred we could only choose just over three hundred for the audience in Mansion House. The audience contribute so much to the atmosphere for the show, so we were delighted that people wanted to be part of it.

After the programme was shown, Tyrone Productions asked me if I would be interested in doing a series of the programmes that would go out weekly, and I was totally gobsmacked.

'Don't get too excited,' I told myself, realizing that the whole approach was just a pitch, and the idea would have to be presented to RTÉ to see if they wanted to take us on.

Also, I was very aware that my tour schedule was pretty mental for 2016 and I had no idea how I would fit filming in, bearing in mind that we would have to schedule it not only to suit me but also to suit the guests we were hoping to attract to take part in the programme. I was anxious about how it would all work practically but decided to cross that bridge when I came to it. Two months later, Patricia rang me and told me the series had been accepted.

Now came the real work – fitting it into my schedule, for a start! Patricia Carroll, the managing director of Tyrone Productions, calls it her 'Nathan Carter' year, because it really did take over all of their plans. Recruiting guests for four shows, finding an audience to be part of each one . . . and we were due to record the programmes at the end of August. We were in pre-production for about eight weeks for the series, and then we recorded in late August and early September, and then it was straight into the edit as the first programme had to be broadcast within three weeks – oh, and that included the recording of another Christmas special as well!

Our working day would start at 10.30 a.m., when we'd run all the music first and then do pre-camera shots for every song. I'd then go and rehearse my scripts for each act and we'd break for dinner, with the doors opening at 6 p.m., audience in for 7 p.m., start recording a quarter of an hour later and then finish at eleven o'clock that night. They were very long days, and it didn't end there, as we then had to go over scripts for the next day. At least, as these shows were recorded in Sligo, it was a bit handier for me to go home so I was going to my own bed after a hard day's work.

Most of the guests were a joy to work with, though I did hear about one ordering a tuna sandwich and, when it didn't arrive quickly enough, he threw his keys down and said they weren't staying, and another was really tricky – he told the band they weren't playing right and had an awful attitude; he even made my questions sound like they were really difficult, as he played around with the answers. I didn't know where to look, and the whole experience gave me a whole new respect for people like Ryan Tubridy and Graham Norton who do this on a regular basis and often don't know how their guests will behave!

Each interview would last about ten minutes and then would be edited down for the final output. It was so much fun watching them all back.

Billy Ocean was so, so cool. He had grey dreadlocks, and I told him he was the coolest grandad ever (apart from my own Grumps, obviously!). He sang 'When the Going Gets Tough' and 'Love Really Hurts Without You', which brought the house down.

Shane Filan, who has had an incredible career with West-life and who also has a love of country music, was another memorable guest. Shane and I were lined up to play support at the infamous Garth Brooks concerts in Croke Park in 2014 that were cancelled, leaving Garth and the 400,000 people who had bought tickets absolutely heartbroken. Looking back, I'm not sure if I was ready for Croke Park at that time. It would have been nerve-wracking for me to be thrown in at the deep end like that. They say everything happens for a reason so maybe it was just a bit too much too soon and a blessing in disguise for me that they didn't go ahead.

Another highlight for me was the opportunity to sing 'The Living Years' with Paul Carrick. I was so nervous – what a song! But after a run-through with the band I felt more at ease, and I think we cracked it.

The third and most recent Christmas special of *The Nathan Carter Show* was recorded in September 2017 at the magnificent Grand Opera House in Belfast and was shown on both BBC and RTÉ. A lot of effort was put into making it a musical and visual treat for all types of viewers, with music, chat and dance, and it was filmed in front of an enthusiastic nine-hundred-strong audience, including my very proud family: Mum, Dad and, of course, Nan.

The audience was great. It was a whole Christmas mix, with young kids right up to grannies and grandads. It just felt really good from start to finish and, fair play to them, we were singing Christmas songs in September, so it was a bit strange, but they were a really good audience and I think that translated on to the screen.

This time, I performed some very special duets with famous musical guests, including former Spice Girl Melanie C, American singer Curtis Stigers (who my mum and dad really enjoyed), Irish singer Una Healy from pop band The

Saturdays and, last but not least, my brother, Jake, with whom I had a bit of light-hearted banter. The audience seemed to really enjoy the family link with Jake, and we just got to be ourselves. Even though it was more or less scripted, it allowed us to show some of the cheeky antics we get up to when we get together.

Singing with Melanie was most definitely a childhood dream come true. She was very easy to work with, really lovely, and as we were both from Liverpool, it turned out of course that we had a few mutual friends. Performing the Bryan Adams classic 'Baby When You're Gone' with Mel C was possibly my favourite duet of the whole series, while Curtis Stigers is definitely up there as one of the nicest people I've ever met in the business. He is a joy to follow on Twitter, and I loved how he handled some trolls who were running down the programme by saying how music is an art form and is there to be enjoyed and not compared. Go, Curtis!

Others taking part in the show included the Canadian family group The Fitzgeralds, with their unique blend of traditional music and step-dancing – and Christmas wouldn't be Christmas without a children's choir so I was joined by the St Patrick's Primary School Choir from Drumgreenagh. The County Down schoolchildren were overall winners of the junior section of the BBC Radio Ulster School Choir of the Year in 2016.

I had the honour of working with so, so many people during those recordings, including Mark Feehily of Westlife, Brian Kennedy, Derek Ryan, Bronagh Gallagher, Finbar Furey, Aston Merrigold, Moya Brennan, Martine McCutcheon (who I called Tiffany when back stage, much to her amusement) and Stella Parton, who I made the mistake of calling Dolly during the actual interview. We had to redo the take!

The big question now, of course, is will we get to do it all again? I'd really love to, and I feel like I have grown into the role of presenting, so although my diary is packed tight as it is, I would love to develop the series. Who knows, maybe one day I'll get my dream guest to perform with me – that would be Mr Tom Jones, who I believe has one of the best vocals out there. He is just so cool, and I totally admire his longevity, from his residency in Vegas to judging *The Voice*. I'd so love to sing 'The Green, Green Grass of Home' with him. Now that would be a duet to remember!

Tyrone Productions also gave me a further crack of the whip with a one-off special called *Nathan Goes to Nashville*. The programme did exactly what it says on the tin – I went to Nashville with my guitarist JP, and we explored the nightlife, the studios, the famous landmarks, such as the Grand Ole Opry; the Ryman Auditorium, where I accompanied Larry Gatlin by adding harmony to his downbeat classic 'All the Gold in California'; the Bridgewater Arena; and the Bluebird Café, where I also got to sing. Having watched and loved the TV series *Nashville*, I was totally bricking it. Thank goodness no one had a clue who I was! There are only ninety people allowed into the Bluebird at any one time, and there were three hundred other people waiting outside, hoping to get in, so I guess it was an honour to have been able to get in through the doors, never mind get to sing a song!

Nathan Goes to Nashville was a documentary, so it wasn't as staged as the TV shows were and it allowed me just to be me while JP and I strolled around and met all sorts of interesting individuals. It was a gruelling schedule, with a sixteen-hour day for the seven days of the week we were there. We ended up with enough footage for two episodes.

One of the highlights of this show, which I thoroughly enjoyed, despite the tough demands on our time, was meeting

Johnny Cash's only son, John Carter Cash, whose wealth is estimated at a whopping $200 million (I wonder are we related . . . ?).

We travelled to meet him, driving through huge gates and beyond his mansion to the log cabin where the late Johnny Cash finally found peace, and he told me of his father's love for Ireland.

'He got there, he saw how beautiful it was, he saw the history that was right there to be seen and he was connected, of course, by blood,' John told me. 'My father has Irish blood, but he is also connected by his heart and by the love for a beautiful, beautiful place and fine, kind people.'

He went on to tell me the story behind his father's famous hit '40 Shades of Green' and how it led to a cherished moment with President John F. Kennedy, and I couldn't resist but have a go at the song myself on the old piano in the log cabin, which was quite a thrill!

I'm nearly sure there's a family tree of mine that says June Carter is a long-lost relative . . .

On our seven-day journey around Music City, on the strip we also met a man known as the Rhinestone Rembrandt who made suits for the stars, including John Travolta and Frank Sinatra – although, at the time, he didn't know who Sinatra was until the great man tipped him a cool $1,000!

I met the legendary Crystal Gayle and got to sing a duet with her on her famous song, 'Don't It Make My Brown Eyes Blue', and got to record with some of the finest musicians in a Nashville studio.

And no trip to Nashville would be complete without a stop-off at the very famous Gruhn's Music Shop, where guitars have been made for the likes of Eric Clapton, Neil Young, Johnny Cash, Lyle Lovett, Vince Gill, George Harrison and Paul McCartney, to name just a few. Needless to say, JP was in his glory, and it was only slightly marred by the fact that we'd been out the night before until the wee hours, not realizing that we had a very early start the next morning for filming. Or maybe I did know but just forgot to tell him . . .

The feedback from the Nashville documentary really blew me away. I felt within myself that it was something special, but I hadn't known what to expect from the viewing public. I'd been told that the average viewing figures for this slot were between 190,000 and 280,000 and, even though I had so many positive comments on social media and from people when I was out and about, it was still a great surprise when the ratings came in: 331,000 viewers had tuned in.

For any country singer, Nashville is the Holy Grail, and I had a ball exploring the famous city and meeting some of its characters. I got a taster of what it might be like to one day perform there in my own right. Or to perform in America for real . . . now that would be another dream come true.

I came home to Ireland full of ideas, hopes and plans and itching to get to know the States even better.

19. In America

The year 2016 had brought me and my band to England, Scotland and even as far away as Australia, where we did a brief four-night promotional tour in Brisbane, Melbourne, Sydney and Perth. Back at home, I was presented with a fantastic opportunity to keep close to my fans through a weekly news column in the Irish newspaper *Sunday World*. I write about what I've been up to, the people I've met and the places I've been, and I've always had plenty to talk about ever since then.

I spent my twenty-seventh birthday in style with a headline show at the London Palladium, and what a night that was! It was a bank-holiday weekend so everyone was in great form and the atmosphere couldn't have been any better. The minute it was over, I was mad to do it again. To book the Palladium, you normally need to be thinking at least eighteen months ahead, so I was delighted to see there was one date in the diary free within that timeframe – and imagine my excitement when I saw it was 17 March 2018, St Patrick's Day! We booked it immediately and, after all that, to reach out to and crack an American audience would truly be the icing on the cake.

My mum's sister, my aunty Siobhan, used to live in Washington DC and, when I was just six years old, we went to visit her and her husband, Van. I remember being mesmerized by how huge everything seemed in this faraway city when we got there, and the magic of Disneyland, where we stayed as part of our trip.

Aunty Siobhan lived in the States for many years and her daughter, Savannah, was born there, so it was always exciting to hear from our American family, especially when Van's parents posted us across some taped recordings of a country-music show from America on a radio station called WMZQ.

WMZQ, which is home to the famous *Bobby Bones Show*, played all the artists I followed, like Tim McGraw, Brad Paisley and Rascal Flatts, and I loved to listen into the ads that would be played between songs for random things like trucks, jerky meat and even guns! I knew every ad off by heart and I used to look forward to hearing all the new songs that would come my way – and the ads, as I was so into trucks and American cars like Chevrolets and Corvettes. When those tapes arrived, it was like a little piece of heaven coming through the postbox, and we'd play them on every car journey, no matter if it was a long run somewhere or a trip to the local shops.

I'd hear and discover lots of new artists from the WMZQ tapes, and it would always help me with my Christmas wish list. I'd request albums from Garth Brooks, The Dixie Chicks and Shania Twain, all of whom I would never have known so well if it hadn't been for those tapes.

Even though I'd always loved music and songs, those tapes and the music they brought my way really inspired me, and my love for country music grew from there, so thanks to Van and his family for sending them my way.

As I listened to those songs, I'd often dream of what it would be like to perform in the United States. It was a place that seemed so out of reach, just a dream, one that was so far away and would never happen. I'd dream of the CMA Festival in Nashville, and of Bridgestone Arena there. The posters outside it were a larger-than-life who's who of country-music royalty.

As my career in Ireland took off, I had the opportunity of

seeing the Bridgestone Arena in all its glory in real life when I took a trip out there to write some songs and do some recording. There's something about the place – it's like a totally different buzz: creativity seeps out of every corner along the strip and everywhere you turn. There's excitement in the air as you imagine the people who sit in the cafés, who play music in the bars and all the opportunities that come their way if they are heard by the right people at the right time.

Garth Brooks was discovered, legend has it, while playing at a singer-songwriter session in a local café there; Taylor Swift was too and, no matter what bar you go into, there's that great rush of wonder, as you never really know who you might be sitting next to.

My songwriting sessions took place at Major Bob Music House, a place run by Garth Brooks' manager, Bob Doyle, where many songwriters are employed full time to work on songs with a range of different artists. I spent two days there and penned a song with John Farry and J. P. Williams called 'Stay Alive', which featured on my 2016 album *Livin' the Dream*. It was such a jaw-dropping experience to work right in the heart of Nashville, where the sounds of those old tapes sent all the way from Van's parents originated, and I continued to dream about one day performing my music to an American audience on my own tour.

Then, in September 2017, when I was twenty-seven years old, it happened.

Our very first, eleven-date North American and Canadian tour took in cities including Detroit, Philadelphia, Chicago, Pittsburgh, Milwaukee, Kingston, Rochester, Davenport, Medford and Wisconsin Dells. Before it all kicked off, I travelled to America, where I met up with Chloe Agnew, a singer from Dublin who was once part of the Celtic Woman group of singers and who would be accompanying me on tour.

Chloe, who has a soprano range vocally, is probably one of the finest singers I have ever had the pleasure of working with, and she has lots of experience of American audiences, having performed with Celtic Woman for ten years, recording fourteen albums with them and taking part in several world tours. Irish audiences may know her as the daughter of Adele 'Twink' King, who is also a singer and entertainer and well known from the girl band Maxi, Dick and Twink from the 1960s and '70s.

Chloe and I met up two months before the beginning of the tour Stateside and appeared on several PBS Pledge local stations to try and garner some interest for our forthcoming shows. In preparation for launching into the US, I had also recorded an album of classic Celtic tunes including 'Caledonia', 'Grace' (featuring Chloe Agnew) and 'Loch Lomond', American ballads 'Bridge over Troubled Water', and 'Hard Times', and a mix of my own hits from down the years, such as 'Where I Wanna Be' and, of course, 'Wagon Wheel'.

As well as the PBS stations, we also went on some daytime TV shows, which was great fun. It was nice to have Chloe there to bounce off, as she knew the market a lot better than I did.

Going to America with my music was a bit like starting all over again, as I was a total stranger to this new audience, but it was very reassuring when three of the dates sold out. Some others weren't so good, but those dates were a great vote of confidence, as we were trying to break into a whole new market where no one had heard of Nathan Carter.

The week before we set off I got a phone call from Daniel O'Donnell, who was in America on his own tour. Daniel kindly suggested I should record a little video about my tour and said that he would play it during the intermission of his current shows there to let people know I was on my way over. This was a great help in spreading the word and I really appreciated his efforts to help me in that way.

The US and Canadian audiences were very receptive to my music and they all seemed very grateful that we had travelled all the way from Ireland to be there. The majority of the audiences were US or Canadian people who liked Irish music, while others were of Irish descent who had been told by their relatives back home to come along and check us out. Chloe brought her own following too, which really helped, and they enjoyed her Celtic ballad performances, which added a new edge to our set list.

The tour bus we had in America was a lot smaller than the one we use back home, so travel arrangements were a bit challenging from time to time. Instead of a double decker with beds upstairs like we are used to, our US bus was all on the same level and, instead of bunkbeds with two beds, these had three, so the top bunk was very high off the ground and the bottom one was very low to the ground! And Chloe was the only girl on the bus with twelve men! After our first gig in America, we didn't realize that we were travelling across the border into Canada during the night, which led to a rather unexpected experience at the checkpoint in the wee hours, as some of us had had quite a bit to drink!

We were so thrilled with the first gig that the moment we got on the bus we cracked open a few beers and enjoyed them while travelling along the American highways, reminiscing on a job well done.

Chloe had long gone on to bed when at 3 a.m. the bus was stopped at Customs and we were asked to get off so it could be checked.

'Is there anyone else on the bus?' asked one of the officials, having counted and checked all twelve of us band and crew off.

'Chloe!' we remembered, realizing that she had been sleeping through all the commotion.

The customs official was quite surprised when Chloe came off the bus, half asleep, and he commended her on sharing a bus with so many merry males who were obviously enjoying a bit of a party along the journey!

The high bunks on the bus were five and a half feet off the ground, so it was a bit dangerous, to say the least, especially when a few drinks were on the scene, and this proved quite a challenge to tour manager Barney Curran, who managed to fall out of his not once, not twice, but a grand total of three times during the trip. He was black and blue by the time he got home to Donegal over a week later!

In America, Barney provided a lot of off-stage entertainment, as he still does to this day, no matter where he goes, in particular when it comes to explaining to inquisitive folk what he does for a living when we aren't on tour.

'I'm a shamrock farmer,' he'd tell them with a straight face.

'You mean clover?' most people would ask him.

'No! Don't ever mention the word "clover" in my company,' he'd joke. 'Clover has the potential to put me out of business. It's three leaves I deal in, not four. I provide all the shamrocks for St Patrick's Day from my farm in Donegal, where the land is worked by my little workforce.'

'You mean you actually employ *leprechauns*?' people would ask, wide-eyed.

'Don't be silly, there's no such thing as leprechauns!' Barney would tell them, and so the spoof would go on. We'd be in stitches laughing until his gathered audience would realize that he was taking the mick.

We have many laughs when we're on tour and we certainly did know how to enjoy ourselves on the American trip. After each show we would host a gathering for some of the punters and promoters who had made it all possible, and I was delighted to meet up with songwriter Joe McShane and his family when we visited Chicago, plus, Chloe was able to meet some friends she knew along the way too.

The best gig of the trip by far was in Boston, where we played to a sell-out audience, thanks to Oran McGonagle, a young guy from Donegal who moved there five or six years ago and who now runs a few Irish-themed bars around the city, including Emmet's Pub, 6B, Carrie Nation, Scholars and Magnolia. When Oran found out we were going to be in the States, he booked us to play in a place called the Chevalier Theatre. He worked really hard to pack the place, and he did. I couldn't believe the amount of people from Donegal and Dublin that turned up, but to be honest, I think most of the counties of Ireland were represented that night.

Oran also looks after a nightclub in Boston, which we thoroughly enjoyed attending afterwards, especially when Barney and I discovered the 'fireball' shots. They went down a treat.

When I think of American country music, it really reminds me of where I want to be in my career. The market out there is something I am intent on focusing on over the next few years. Our introduction to North America and Canada was an eventful one, and we came away from it all feeling refreshed and enthusiastic about going back again, which we plan to do later in 2018 and for many years to come.

I also have noticed that, since that tour, a lot of people who came to see us have joined in on social media and are eager for our return, which is a fantastic sign and shows we must have done something right. I do know that the people there really did enjoy the mix of country and Irish, so it's something we will definitely keep bringing their way and, hopefully, our audience will continue to grow, just like it did back in Ireland.

With an American tour now under my belt, I had achieved one of my biggest ambitions and I'd proven to myself that even my wildest dreams really could come true. But I have so many still to fulfil . . .

20. *Livin' the Dream*

The years 2016 and 2017 were amazing years all round, with Australia, the North American and Canadian tour, the *Nathan Carter* TV show on RTÉ, the Christmas special on RTÉ and BBC, plus, we sold out the London Palladium at two thousand seats that night of my twenty-seventh birthday and the people there said they'd never seen the like of it, with the audience up out of their seats dancing during the first song.

The Cork Marquee events were another 'pinch me' moment when, for two years in a row, we'd performed on the same bill as some of the world's biggest stars. The first time, in 2016, we were on the same weekend as Imelda May and Little Mix, while in 2017 we were sandwiched between Bryan Adams, Gavin James and Emeli Sandé.

I honestly thought that things couldn't get any bigger in such a short space of time, but they did.

Livin' the Dream was the biggest-selling album in Ireland in June 2017, going straight to number one, and what was even more of a thrill for me was that it sat up there just above one of my favourite artists, superstar Ed Sheeran.

After all those weeks at number one, Ed finally moved over and let me have my turn at the top spot! My fans came through for me and pushed me over the line into that top position, and I couldn't believe it. We set off out on the road to sign copies of the album and I was delighted to see people of all ages turn up. One fan even bringing along a little puppy called Tiny to say hello. That's the best thing about my fans – you just never know who or what you will come across sometimes.

The year of 2017 was when I got to build bridges with one of my heroes. Yes, the accordion player Mick Foster of Foster and Allen! I've been lucky enough to get to know Mick and his equally talented performing partner, Tony Allen, and the idea to get together on a song, 'Burning Bridges', like most good ideas, started off in a pub.

We were at a Charlie Landsborough concert in the Grand Opera House in Belfast and afterwards we all went for a drink in a bar across the road for a catch-up. Tony had come up with the idea of covering the Status Quo classic, which the band had performed on their acoustic tour with two accordions. Foster and Allen have one accordion player, of course . . . now who could they get to be their second for this extra-special recording?

Me, of course, and for me, it doesn't get any better than playing with Foster and Allen, so I jumped at the chance. We filmed a video for the song in Belfast around iconic landmarks including the Titanic Quarter and also on Derry's Peace Bridge, which was great fun.

Mick and Tony really are a joy to hang out with – they are two great characters, and Mick is one of the funniest people you'll ever meet. He's just a natural comic, and he isn't even aware of it. We joked when we were filming outside Queen's in Belfast that it was the closest any of us would ever get to gaining a university degree!

From Belfast to Derry with Foster and Allen, 2017 also brought me to the beautiful town of Tralee in County Kerry, where I was part of the famous International Rose of Tralee festival. It's one of my favourite Irish festivals and is among the largest and longest running in the country – I suppose you might say it's the festival equivalent of television's *The*

Late Late Show, as far as popularity goes! I had an absolute ball, as always, performing at the festival, and it's such an honour to be asked to return year after year to take part in such a memorable event.

Another first for me in 2017 was being invited by Peter Aiken of Aiken Promotions to play Iveagh Gardens in Dublin along with a stellar line-up of performers including Aslan, Olly Murs, Damien Dempsey, Passenger and many more, but the biggest thrill was when Peter told me that I was the first country artist ever to play there.

Iveagh Gardens are often referred to as the Secret Gardens of Dublin, as they are in a great location but thousands of people walk past them every day without even knowing they exist. Since I'd always associated events there with indie, rock and pop groups, I was chuffed to bits that I was doing something that was not only a first for myself but also a first for country music. Luckily, apart from some drizzle at one point, the unpredictable Irish weather was on its best behaviour for a change, which made it an even better experience than I could have expected, and the mixed-age audience totally entered into the spirit of things. Among the audience was none other than Hollywood actor Patrick Bergin of *Sleeping with the Enemy* fame and now a familiar face in the British TV soap *EastEnders*. I got chatting with Patrick afterwards, and it turns out he's a true fan of country music and performs and writes himself.

I also had the pleasure to work with Tommy Swarbrigg, a promoter from Mullingar who looks after a large number of our regular Irish gigs, including the Cork Opera House, University Concert Hall in Limerick and the Mullingar Park Hotel.

From the Dalriada Festival in Glenarm, County Antrim, to Holy Cross in Tipperary, where there was a crowd of ten thousand, the summer of 2017 was one high after another, but the real highlight of the year had happened a few months before that, and it was something I never thought in my wildest dreams would happen. We had decided on an ambitious takeover of Ireland's two biggest venues – the SSE Arena in Belfast and the 3Arena in Dublin.

The idea came about one night in Glasgow after a gig when we were having a beer, and it was Tom Sheerin, our fiddle player, who brought it up.

'You should look into the two Irish arenas,' Tom said.

I almost choked on my drink. 'You think?'

The thought had crossed my mind before, but I never thought it would be possible so soon.

'Sure,' said Tom. 'You should believe in yourself more. You have the profile, you're packing them in all over Ireland. I think it might work.'

The seed was planted, and I broached the subject with John Farry, who agreed to run it by Peter Aiken of Aiken Promotions.

We'd worked with Peter on a few occasions, selling out the Bord Gáis Energy Theatre in Dublin, as well as two nights at the renowned Vicar Street venue.

'It should work,' said Peter. 'I have no reason to believe that it wouldn't, especially with the ratings that the TV shows have pulled in.'

This was a huge vote of confidence, coming as it did from one of the country's leading promoters, but did he really think we could do it? No country artist in Ireland, apart from Daniel O'Donnell twenty years ago, had done this. It was a big gamble, or was it? Peter didn't think so.

'At the very least, you could play half-halls in each venue,' he explained. What he meant by this was that the audience capacity can be reduced to about five thousand in Dublin

Crystal Gayle and myself backstage at the Grand Ole Opry, Nashville

Corona v. Guinness – ?? LOL

Brad Paisley and I, backstage at the 3 Arena, Dublin

Legend Johnny
McEvoy and myself at
his show at the
Ardhowen Theatre,
Enniskillen, 2017

The *Sunday World*
Awards, 2017:
Eddie Rowley,
myself and Father
Brian D'Arcy

Checking out a cool car in Nashville, June 2016

It's a pity we didn't all go to school there … On the video shoot for 'Burning Bridges' with Mick Foster and Tony Allen

Me on stage with Grumps at the Liverpool Philharmonic Theatre, September 2016

Just about to go on stage at the Royal Concert Hall in Glasgow, November 2016

Daniel O'Donnell and I on stage in Dungloe, August 2017

With Alex Jones and Matt Baker from BBC's *The One Show*

Fundraiser event, Letterkenny, August 2017: Daniel, Big Tom (RIP), myself and Dominic Kirwan

All round to Mrs Brown's! LOL: Brendan O'Carroll and myself

Live on stage with Shane Filan on *The Nathan Carter Show*

With the legend Paul Carrick on *The Nathan Carter Show*

With Martine McCutcheon on the set of *The Nathan Carter Show*

and four and a half thousand in Belfast if we didn't sell out the maximum, which is anything up to ten thousand tickets. As much as playing even to a half-hall capacity got me excited, I couldn't help but dream of what it might be like to really pack the place out with ten thousand people! What a dream come true that would be!

He advised us not to take on smaller venues so that the two big ones would work, and this sounded like common sense, so we put our necks on the line and put the tickets out on sale to see how they would go.

Both these iconic venues are places where I'd seen some of my favourite artists perform – Ed Sheeran, Lionel Richie, Brad Paisley and Dolly Parton, to name a few – so could I really get up on the same stage there on my own show? By now I'd outsold One Direction, Pharrell Williams and even Michael Bublé in Ireland, plus, my latest album release, *Livin' the Dream*, had followed suit and gone to number one, so we just went for it, inviting Sharon Shannon and her band along to do both gigs with us.

When I saw my name on billboards while driving through Belfast I couldn't believe my eyes. And then the same in Dublin . . . I always enjoy going to the annual Country to Country festival at the 3Arena and, when I went along and saw The Dixie Chicks, Lady Antebellum and Brad Paisley play to a half-full arena, my nerves were in bits. If they couldn't fill the hall, then perhaps we were ambitious to even think that doing so might be a possibility for us?

I waited in anticipation and, within three months, Dublin had sold out. The same happened in Belfast, about a week before we opened there. We didn't have to consider half-halls after all – we'd sold out the biggest indoor arenas in Ireland. It was a massive milestone in an already tremendous year.

As the countdown began in the week leading up to the event, we rehearsed in a warehouse in Dunboyne, County Meath, where we put up the full rig and got used to working with the seventeen musicians who would be on stage with me on the night. To add to the pressure, I'd decided to record the 3Arena show for a DVD – and you already know what I'm like when I know there are cameras recording! I could end up coming out with anything and embarrassing myself!

The gigs themselves were electric, and it was a feeling I wish I could bottle up and keep.

To walk out on stage to almost ten thousand people in a country that had adopted me as one of its own, with my parents, grandparents and close friends watching on closely, was a moment that I didn't ever think I would be able to top. The sound of the crowd cheering, the beat of the band, who played an absolute blinder, and the warmth of the atmosphere was a powerful force of energy that pushed my adrenaline higher than I ever imagined it could go.

'You're living the dream,' many people had said to me lately (hence the name of my latest album), and on those two stages in Belfast and Dublin, I really was doing just that.

One highlight for me at the Belfast arena gig was when I had to find an audience member, Stefan Green, who had a question to ask his girlfriend, Louise Lovett. Yes, you guessed right, there was a proposal! I returned to the piano onstage and sang 'Good Morning Beautiful' for the happy couple.

In Dublin, the best part of the show for me was when I brought in John Sheahan from The Dubliners and we sang 'The Rare Auld Times' and the audience clapped for over two minutes after it. To have that moment with John, the last remaining Dubliner, was really something special. It was magical, a unique moment, and the crowd went wild.

As the audience applauded and applauded and I looked

across at one of the finest, most well-respected and renowned Irish performers, I thought of how I used to listen to The Dubliners as a young child with my grandparents and sing along as I rode in the back of Nan's car.

Now, here I was – in Ireland, in front of a massive crowd of people who had come to see me, singing with one of the people I had long admired. I just couldn't believe it.

The year continued on a high, as we visited the Costa del Sol in October for what has now become an annual country-music pilgrimage to the town of Benalmádena, where we were joined by lots of familiar faces, including fans, friends and fellow country-music singers for a week of partying, jiving and craic.

Benalmádena is a town of 'bright lights and vibrant nights' and, with its Mediterranean temperatures, it certainly is the perfect spot for some dancing with a difference, and a welcome change from the blustery weather of Ireland and Britain.

We've had lots of adventures on the Costa over the past couple of years, some more memorable than others, and although we always have a ball, I do recall one concert over there when the weather went totally against us and it was more like a wet day in Bundoran than anything you'd expect in Benalmádena!

We were all set up for an outdoor concert on the beautiful terraces of the hotel. The mood was perfect, all our sound and lighting equipment and instruments were in place and the merry crowd were gathering for some sun-soaked country-music fun – but we ended up getting a soaking of a very different type!

Just when the host, Hugo Duncan, was announcing the first act of the evening, it began to rain ever so slightly – just a light spit, you might say – and we were all whispering in the wings, trying not to panic and praying that it would stop within a few minutes, but oh no – it got a hundred times worse and the heavens burst open. We stood there in shock as we watched the rain bounce off the terraces, and the audience ran for cover into the hotel. We grabbed what we could, including the new star cloth backdrop. It was so heavy wet that it took three people to lift it. I was honestly about to cry as I saw everything swimming in puddles, and we had to buy two very expensive fans to dry all of the equipment out.

Thankfully, the rain in Spain does stay mainly on the plain, and we've never looked back, as the Carter on the Costa is now at a new venue, where we can go and properly let our hair down each year. The 'busman's holiday' is now organized by Enjoy Travel, who I spent that first cruise with back in 2006 and with whom I now enjoy (pardon the pun!) a very strong working relationship. It's a super time of year to get away from it all and I love to get the chance to hang out with lots of different country singers, which, this year, included Philomena Begley, Cliona Hagan, Lisa McHugh, Johnny Brady, Barry Kirwan, Hugo Duncan and lots more. We had lots of laughs and late nights, with Philomena joining me on stage into the wee hours to do a duet of 'Blanket on the Ground', much to the delight of everyone who was up late enough to sing along!

As 2017 came to a close and the long winter nights drew in, I took the longest break I've had in a long time, and kicked back and relaxed with a family Christmas spent, for the very first time, in Fermanagh. With Jake starring in panto in Belfast, it meant he couldn't take time out to go to Liverpool, as we always did – so Liverpool came to us and we had a ball. And I managed not to poison anyone with my turkey, which I served with all the trimmings (okay, I'll admit it – Mum helped . . . a lot!). I also managed not to set off any smoke alarms or burn the spuds, which was my biggest fear.

We spent time at the Christmas markets in Belfast, watched the Christmas special from the Grand Opera House on TV, we cheered, booed and hissed along with Jake at the panto in the SSE Arena and we ate and drank till we were merry, reliving memories of family Carter Christmases past.

It was a nice change all round to have my wonderful family in Fermanagh with us, as it just wouldn't be Christmas without them, and after a week of fun I waved them all off as they set off for home, as always, with mixed emotions, but knowing it wouldn't be long until we met up again.

As the New Year rolled in and snow lay thick on the ground in Fermanagh, I was itching to get back to work, as my 2018 UK tour beckoned at the end of the month.

That year had been amazing, full of new career highs and bigger milestones than I could ever have imagined, and now a whole new twelve months of action-packed adventures lay ahead.

Eventually, my bags were packed, the rehearsals were done and I woke up in the still of the winter blackness to the shrill sound of my early-morning alarm.

It was dark, I was tired and, when it dawned on me as I woke up that it was tour time, I felt nerves – good nerves, familiar nerves – twitch in my stomach.

It was tour time again and I honestly couldn't wait to get stuck in.

PART TWO
Born for the Road

'What happens on tour, stays on tour.'

It's one of the most notorious sayings in show business, and means that whatever happens on the road must be kept top secret, but I'm going to break that rule ever so slightly and share with you some of what we get up to when we travel up and down the country and beyond as we bring the Nathan Carter show to your doorstep.

We have had many incidents that maybe *should* be kept quiet, and many belly laughs along the way that will stay with me for ever, like the time when Barney, Gareth and I went for a few drinks after a show in Aberdeen and slowly wandered back to the tour bus, only to find it had already moved on! When we rang JP it turned out they were forty miles into their journey and hadn't even noticed we weren't there. The bus had to stop and wait, and we had to get a very expensive taxi to go and meet them, trying the patience of the driver to no end, I'm sure. And isn't it nice to see they missed us in the first place . . . ?

On a separate occasion, Barney and I were in Dublin at a ladies' banquet, and the next day we flew to Glasgow to do some CD signings, which were to be followed by a second signing in Liverpool. We hopped on the train to Liverpool from Glasgow, fell asleep and woke up 190 miles away from where we were meant to be. We had to then get a taxi, which cost us £200, and in the rush to get out of it when we finally got to our proper destination Barney forgot his phone, which we had to recover the next day when we were in Manchester – which cost him another £90 for the driver to bring it to him!

We've been put out of McDonald's in America for skipping the queue, and one night in Motherwell in Scotland we got into a bit of trouble in a Premier Inn for being too noisy. We decided after a really good gig that we'd have a few people back for a sing-song and, since Gareth and I had the biggest room, this was the room we chose to go to. The whole band came in, as did the crew, and we put on some music and were having great craic when there was a knock on the door. It was a member of staff who asked us to keep the noise down, as the hotel had a 'shush policy', which meant quiet after a certain time of night. This happened again a second time and, when she came up for the third time, I promised we would definitely be good, but I had the bright idea of putting the mattress from one of the beds up against the door, thinking it would soak up the sound. Of course, this didn't work at all and, eventually, we were all asked to leave the hotel. As it was the early hours of the morning by then, we didn't have anywhere to go, so I begged the management to let the band and crew go back to their rooms and promised that Gareth, Barney and I, who were the main instigators of the sing-song, would go elsewhere, as it was our room and we were the real culprits.

So off we set at 4 a.m. to find another hotel and. since I had no cash on me, Gareth had to fork out £160 for a room ten miles away that we only got to spend about five hours in before it was time to get up and move on to our next venue of the tour!

Of course, all joking aside, when we're on tour we essentially have a massive job to do, and it's not just a matter of turning up at a venue and playing a few tunes, nor is it all about having the craic, though we really do enjoy ourselves as much as we can.

We have a fantastic crew who build our set each day and set up the drums, the piano and all the instruments and microphones and so on that you see on stage in time for our early-evening sound check, and then it's down to business after a quick bite to eat, when we get ready for the two-hour show, which is normally followed by a meet-and-greet with the fans.

The UK tour of early 2018 is kicking off in Billingham, a town in County Durham, but it is planned at least a year in advance, from John Farry's office at home in Garrison, County Fermanagh, where he works with his wife, Anne. From there, John will liaise either directly with the venue, or with a concert promoter, which in this case is Kennedy Street, a company based in Cheshire. He discusses and plans all promotional material, and he will then monitor ticket sales coming up to each event and organize any television and radio opportunities that come my way which will help create a buzz for the shows, plus, any other promotional opportunities that might come about in each town or city that we visit. On completion of the gigs, John will look after the settlement of all the finances, and he attends a lot of the Irish gigs as well as popping across to some of the UK gigs too, to make sure it's all running smoothly.

From that office in Garrison, a network of people, including some of the finest session musicians, who are very sought after across a range of musical genres, come on board to make the tour happen, so, to give you an insight into the fantastic work everyone does to make it all fall into place, let me introduce you to the rest of the team and tell you a little about what they do . . .

Mike McCarthy: promoter's representative

Mike is the promoter's representative on this tour from Kennedy Street. The promoter hires the venue for each gig and it is their responsibility to promote the show through advertising, so all the posters and flyers you see with tour dates will come from their end of things after being agreed by John and me. They also make sure that timetables for each day are set up and adhered to, such as advising the truck and bus drivers where they can park and get power (we need electricity on the tour bus), and where we can all have showers and get changed when we get to each venue. Mike allocates guest-list tickets, he communicates with the box office, and he makes sure that we have all we need in our dressing room (he draws the line at blue M&Ms, though!). Mike has worked with many bands, including 10CC, Mike and the Mechanics, Gladys Knight, Barry Manilow and Neil Sedaka, to name just a few.

'I love the intensity of my job as a promoter,' says Mike. 'It's quite intense for three or four weeks, where I'll work seven days a week for sixteen to eighteen hours, but then I'll have two to three weeks off, which I normally spend in Spain, which is very nice. Every day brings new challenges and my days are always busy, but I do seem to manage to get an hour or so to zone out, which allows me to keep focused. I have to be aware of everything that's going on.

'When on tour I like to bring my iPad, my iPod and my laptop so I can watch BBC iPlayer when we have some downtime, and I always bring a good book.'

And the downsides of life on the road?

'It can be hard to find some personal space and to arrange all your own "stuff", but I've got a system that keeps me right. I take three bags – wardrobe management is very important in my job, as I have to deal with people all the time and therefore have to try and look presentable, which isn't always easy when living on a bus! Sometimes it can be a bit messy and, when you get to a venue and their internet is very slow or not working, it can be very annoying!'

Barney Curran: tour manager

Barney looks after a lot of the on-the-ground stuff when we're on the road for this tour. He has a few roles – everything from ironing shirts and looking after my wardrobe to managing the meet-and-greet after each show. Barney assists with travel and accommodation and deals with front-of-house issues, including anything that might arise from audience members.

'It's great working with Nathan,' says Barney, 'and I love how he always has time for people, and that means everyone, from babies to grannies! He is a real credit to his parents, though he does get some bad habits from Nan, for example, losing his phone and car keys!!

'It's never about the last gig with Nathan, it's about the next one. It's never about the last song, it's about the next one. This is what he was born to do and I'm so honoured to be a part of it on this tour.'

Derek Reilly: production manager

When tour time comes round, Derek drives the truck that holds all our equipment, which means that he works very long hours and he definitely doesn't have time to party, like some of us do! Before we head off on tour, I get pictures in my head of what I want the stage to look like and I discuss this with Derek, who never lets me down when it comes to production ideas, so he's a man of many talents. He has great experience on the road, having worked on Eurovision tours and with many other Irish acts.

'The crew start to unload the truck each day around

lunchtime,' says Derek, 'and they have everything in place by 4.30 p.m. that day. I get great job satisfaction from working with Nathan, and I only ever have to go back to him if there's a really big problem. Thankfully, that doesn't happen very often.

'The only downside is the lack of sleep, which I make sure and catch up on when I get home!'

James Enevoldson: front-of-house sound engineer

James, who is from Leeds but now lives in Liverpool, makes sure that every member of the audience at a Nathan Carter show hears the music the way we want them to. He looks after the sound desk, the speakers and all the microphones on stage and monitors the sound, adjusting it if necessary throughout the performance for every single song. James has worked with acts including Heather Small, The Three Degrees and The Real People.

'We tour our own PA, which is set up in each venue accordingly, and I decide what mics are used for each instrument,' says James. 'Nathan has his preference for sound and he takes a lot of interest, which I really like. He has invested in high-quality gear and is a good collaborator, which always makes for a better show. I work closely with Martin and Craig, who help me rig up the PA. Martin looks after radio mics and plugs them all in onstage, so I rely heavily on him, while Craig sets up all the instruments.

'I always aim for crystal-clear sound and for Nathan's voice to shine and, with forty-eight sound inputs to be balanced, we aim for a CD-type sound. I know what it takes to make a band sound good and, as it's such a big responsibility, my heart starts racing as soon as the show starts as the adrenaline and nerves kick in. When it starts, for me, there is no rush like it, and the high you feel after a gig has gone well is a great feeling.

'I love the day-to-day challenge of the job and the family atmosphere that comes with being part of the Nathan Carter show. I do feel tired a lot of the time, but it's all worth it! I've been all over the world doing this job now, and I feel lucky to be doing it. Everyone at home always loves to hear all about what I do, so it's certainly not a boring job at all.

'I know every solo of every instrument, every vocal, and I have to be totally on the ball to keep making the necessary changes to keep it all at the highest standards. Nathan really looks after the team and takes such an interest in everything that's going on and, for me, it's that, his star quality and his voice, that make it all such a great success.'

John 'JP' Pettifer: musical director/guitar player

JP is one of the finest session musicians out there and is the backbone of the band in his role as musical director. It's his job to put all the songs together, to hire and fire band members and to liaise with TV shows when we're performing with special guests to make sure that everyone knows what they're doing. JP also accompanies me to any radio or TV promotions, as they are very often acoustic and it will be just me and him, and we travel further afield a lot together, for example, we're going to Germany and America soon to set up some promos for gigs there later in the year. JP has been with me for five years and, before that, this fellow Scouser who now lives near me in Fermanagh played in Charlie Landsborough's band.

'I absolutely love the live shows,' says J P. 'The gigs are just fantastic. To get paid for something you really love is something I never take for granted, as I know many people who work nine to five and who live for the weekend. For me, it's the opposite. I don't particularly enjoy the "on the road" living, as it's hard to live out of a case on a bus, but the moment you step on to the stage it's worth it all.

'The TV shows are a great challenge when we have to coordinate four shows in one session, rehearsing, playing and recording them all in the same day, but it all comes good in the end.

'We have great fun on the road and love to play the odd prank – Nathan is absolutely petrified of rats, he has a phobia of them, and sometimes we put a fake rat inside the piano so that he'll see it when he lifts the cover to play a song. He's been known to really scream and let out a few choice words, jumping about six feet in the air with fear when he sees it. We pulled one across the stage once and it scared the life out of him!

'Nathan is one of the boys. He never comes across as the boss and never demands any special treatment when we're on the road. He gets the drinks in, makes sure everyone is looked after and is very easy-going, which I think is down to his great upbringing. Any Scouser who gets above themselves will always get knocked back down again, but Nathan never gets uppity at all. He's done the rounds, he's played the pubs and weddings, and he knows how lucky he is now to be at the top of his game. This is something he appreciates, which not everyone who reaches his heights of fame does. He knows where he came from and where he is now and is very happy and content.

'Nathan is a good lad and he makes me very proud. Yes, I'm not afraid to say that. He makes me very, very proud.'

Gareth Lowry: drummer

Gareth, who is from Castlederg in County Tyrone, is the longest-serving member of the Nathan Carter band, having been on the road with me now for eight years, as well as playing with many other bands on the country scene as a session drummer. His dad also plays in country bands and his cousin plays with well-known folk band The Logues.

'I love the atmosphere of life on the road, the camaraderie and the craic,' says Gareth. 'We are a very relaxed bunch compared to other bands, and everyone gets on really well. Nathan is very down to earth and approachable, and he spends time with everyone – as well as being exceptionally musical, he is also very genuine on a personal level, and my mum loves him! He always hugs her and she has a lot of time for him.

'My daughter Abbie is also a big fan, as Nathan is her god-father, and that's the hardest thing about being on the road – I do miss home a lot and I spend a lot of time on the phone to my fiancée, Emma, sometimes for an hour at a time, but the good side is that when we are not touring I might be at home for three weeks straight, which allows for a lot of quality time.

'I know I could approach Nathan for anything. He's been so good to me and is so loyal – he's a really good friend and is always there, be it to go for a quiet pint or for a bit of lunch and a chat.

'We have many funny memories, and I remember one night when a fan collapsed during a performance of the single "One for the Road", and everyone gathered round him, very concerned, but when he saw Nathan come close to him he was well enough to ask for a free CD! We really do see it all, and one night in the very early days we even found a girl crouching down in the back of the car when we went to go home, and she refused to get out for a long time!

'I also remember he let me down a bagful one night in Castlederg by ordering a pint of Guinness with blackcurrant in it, which could only come from an Englishman! He got a lot of abuse over that one for a very long time.

'Nathan and I are great friends both on and off the road, and I think so highly of him that I even asked him to be my best man. I don't think I can speak of him any higher than that, as that says it all.'

Carl Harvey: bass

Carl, who is from Belfast, has been with the band for two years. He has played with the Lisa McHugh band as well as the Ulster Orchestra and continues to play with many rock bands, making him a very versatile and talented musician.

'My working day begins with the sound check in the afternoon, unless we've any media interviews to attend before that, and then it's food, the gig and I'm in bed as soon as I can and I watch Netflix.

'I really enjoy playing with such a good band, and it's great to get to see so many different places when you're on the road. I've been to places I never thought I'd see, including Dubai, Australia, America and France. It's great to hang out with the band and everyone is great company. I was told by a friend that, twenty years ago, most touring musicians brought a laptop and DVDs to keep themselves entertained, but now we've all downsized, of course, and all I take is my iPad and I can download whatever I want to watch.

'Back home I live with three mates and a dog. We're a

good unit as we all play music together, and we've a studio in the house, which means there isn't a day that goes by that we aren't playing music of some sort, so when I'm on the road I have to leave that all behind and it's a part of life that I enjoy a lot.

'Sleeping on the bus can be tricky but, apart from that, I don't mind it at all. Nathan knows his music so well and has learned so much from being on the job. He takes an interest in all elements and he has an annoying amount of energy, but he isn't afraid to get stuck in, which makes it great to work with him.'

John Byrne: saxophone, keyboards, whistles, backing vocals

John is from a very musical family, and he has been with the Nathan Carter band for just over two years, as well as working as a composer and session musician. You can hear his saxophone on many songs and musical compositions recorded in Ireland. John is from Navan, County Meath.

'I have five brothers and one sister, who all play music. Even both my parents write songs. Dad had a wedding band and we all played in it at some stage, which meant that, growing up, I thought that everyone played music! I've been in bands with Jimmy Buckley, Derek Ryan, Michael English, Patrick Feeney, as well as the RTÉ Orchestra and the Ulster Orchestra.

'On the road I bring my laptop so that I can work on other projects between gigs. I like recording and making string and band arrangements, so I get a lot of that done as we travel.

'I enjoy travelling with such high-quality musicians who can play any genre, and that's definitely a big plus in working with this band. However, I have two children at home and my nine-year-old daughter gets very upset when I leave, which makes it hard on me. My fourteen-year-old son doesn't mind so much, but it's still hard being away from them both. For two days before I go, I have to prepare my daughter for me leaving, which normally means bringing her out for a meal or to the cinema, and when I'm away I WhatsApp a lot and call her. She likes to see the bus and know what I'm doing and hear about all the places we visit.

'Nathan is very talented and knows exactly what he is doing, plus, he never sings out of tune. He is a really nice guy and I think that comes across to anyone who meets him. We never have an argument and he's full of craic, even a bit mischievous, like the time we were on *The Late Late Show* performing "Good-time Girls" and I had to take the sax out of my mouth as I couldn't stop laughing at him, and the track was still playing!'

Matthew Curran: guitars, harmonica, backing vocals

Matt is from Derry and he has been with the Nathan Carter band for almost three years. He continues to record and play his own music and he performs with many of the industry's biggest names.

'I have played with many country artists, including Dominic Kirwan, Derek Ryan, Pam Tillis, Colin Raye and Hal Ketchum. I enjoy working with Nathan a lot. He's a really good guy to work with and a fantastic vocalist.'

Tom Sheerin: fiddle, mandolin

Tom is from Athlone in County Meath, where he is a member of a very musical family who all play country music for many artists. He plays fiddle, mandolin and also claims to be the best dancer amongst us!

'I love the banter with the lads on the road, and all of the gigs are a real joy to be part of,' says Tom. 'For me, with three young boys and a wife at home, it is very tough to be away from home so much, sometimes weeks at a time. I try to stay healthy when on tour and I go for a run every morning and, for comfort, I bring ear plugs, which are an essential, as there are a lot of very loud snorers on the bus all at the same time!

'For me, personally, I believe that Nathan is so successful because, apart from being a big star, he is also a fantastic musician. He's a genuine guy, he never treats anyone in the band any differently and I think that's why he has made it this far.'

And that's it! That's the lot of us – so now that you've met the team and know a little bit about them, it's time to tell you how it all comes together and how they all worked to bring the show to different towns and venues across the UK in early 2018.

So come on, jump aboard the tour bus and buckle up – we're going on the road!

First Leg of the UK *Livin'* *the Dream* Tour
(Thursday, 25 January–Monday, 29 January 2018)

After a bleary-eyed breakfast at the airport in Belfast and then the red-eye flight to Newcastle, England, we are glad to see the familiar sight of our tour bus, which is waiting for us when we get off the flight and into the cold, very early-morning January air.

It's been a bitter winter in Ireland, and the weather doesn't seem to be letting up when we get to Newcastle, so I'm glad I don't have a lot to carry as we make our way, shivering, to the bus. The instruments and all the technical equipment, such as staging, sound and lighting, are already on the way to the concert venue in Billingham with Derek, so all I have to look after is a small case that will get me through the weekend.

I'm pretty low maintenance when touring nowadays, so I don't have an awful lot of luggage with me, like I used to have. I've learned now to take what I need and no more. We tour for four or five days at a time (we used to do more, but it was too long without a break), so I have it down to a tee when it comes to packing clothes and take just exactly enough stuff with me to last every day, and I know that if I really do ever get stuck, there's always going to be a high street nearby to grab a change if I manage to spill something down the front of my shirt! (Yes, it has happened before . . .)

Five of us have travelled from Belfast, while the other

six came from Dublin, and we all head straight for the bunk-beds on the first floor of the tour bus to make the most of the forty-minute jaunt to the first venue, Billingham Forum Theatre.

The ground floor of the bus has some booth-like seats with tables (a bit like a train), a small kitchen area with a microwave, fridge and sink, and a toilet (for 'number ones only'), and the second floor sleeps up to fourteen people in bunkbeds which don't leave room for much movement and definitely aren't good for claustrophobic types, but we're all used to it by now and we're delighted to get a bit of a sleep to prepare us for the weekend ahead after such an early start.

We've played this venue twice before and, with six hundred seats, it's one of the smaller venues of the tour, but we're all excited to get onstage, so after a quick power nap I get up for a look around and I'm delighted to bump into the Haley Sisters, Jo-Ann and Becky, plus their guitarist, Brian Smith, who will be our support act on this tour. I've known the girls, who are from Bingley in West Yorkshire, for twelve years now, since they sang backing vocals and harmonies on my very first recording at Redcar Studios. They are fantastic singers and they provide a lovely warm-up act with their mellow and up-tempo sound. They meet me with smiles and hugs, which is just what I need, as I can feel the nerves starting to gather as the opening night of this tour draws closer.

I've quite a lot in my head, so much to remember, and the acoustic set which we've just added on for this tour is really playing on my mind, as we haven't performed it in front of a live audience yet.

After our usual 4.30 p.m. soundcheck, a bite to eat with the lads and a shower and change of clothes, I'm ready to go onstage and, as always, once I get into the swing of it, it's like we never were on a break at all. Out on the merchandise stall, Nan is taking orders for T-shirts, mugs, CDs, calendars – even pillowcases. You name it, if there's room for my name or face on something, Nan will sell it, and it's a real work of art how she sets everything up on display and chats to everyone, even posing for selfies when requested, which is more often than not. I sometimes think that people come to my shows to chat to Nan as much as they come to hear me and the band!

The acoustic set goes down a treat and I manage to remember all the lyrics. In fact, it all goes amazingly and runs very smoothly, with many people commenting afterwards on how much they had enjoyed the new additions to the set list.

I meet some fans afterwards at the meet-and-greet and, when I hear that Nan had driven down from Liverpool to meet us in Billingham on her own, I decide to accompany her back to Liverpool instead of going with the bus, as I don't want her making the journey so late at night by herself, so I see the bus off and make my way with Nan in the car, agreeing to meet up with everyone again the next day in Manchester for the next gig of the tour.

It's so lovely to see Nan again and, for the first time, I get to see her new apartment, which her and Grumps had moved into just a few days before. They'd lived in a granny flat off my mum and dad's house for a few years, but since my parents are selling up, Nan and Grumps have now got their own new pad, and they are delighted with it. I'm not one bit surprised to see that the walls are already covered in framed photos of all of us grandchildren – honestly, if she could fill every inch of the walls with pictures, she would.

I have to say too that it's a real treat to get into a cosy bed instead of my wee bunk on the tour bus and, later, I sleep like a log at my parents' house, exhausted after a very long day. I still have my own room in my mum and dad's house, even though I've never really lived in that actual house with them, and so do my brother and sister, which is nice because when we go to stay we all have our own space and it's just like stepping back in time with Mum and Dad.

The next morning Nan and I are off bright-eyed and bushy-tailed to Blackpool to visit the Hilton Hotel, who will host our big weekend in March. We want to meet the management team who will be looking after us and have a look at the function rooms and see where we would set everything up, like ticket desks, merchandise stalls and all the usual space we need to please the five hundred punters, many of whom are travelling from all over the UK and Ireland to join in on the weekend.

The Hilton Hotel, it turns out, is perfect and lives up to our expectations, which is a great relief. It's a big step up from previous venues and even has a swimming pool, so it's nice to know that those making the effort to be there should be pleased with the standard when they get here. It's my first time hosting my own weekend in Blackpool, and it's important to make sure that all the finer detail is checked over.

We head off afterwards to Manchester's Bridgewater Hall, which is tonight's venue, and as it's a 2,300-seater, it's a much bigger location than the night before. I'm pleased to hear that it's almost sold out, which is fantastic, as it's our first time playing here.

I've made a few adjustments to tonight's set, taking out a few of the slower songs and replacing them with livelier beats, knowing that a Friday-night audience is a different dynamic to a Thursday-night crowd.

John Farry arrives in Manchester before the gig for a quick meeting with Kennedy Street, who are promoting the tour, and we discuss plans for the autumn gigs, which kick off in

September. It seems like a long way off when we have only just started this season, but there is so much planning to be done that we need to get stuck in now.

Showtime comes around and when we go on stage the audience in Bridgewater all seem to be in great form and the gig goes very well from start to finish. After the meet-and-greet, Barney, Gareth and I head off for a few quiet drinks at a local Irish bar – but we should have known it wouldn't be quiet: when we arrive it's full of people from the gig, and they all want photos and selfies. The lads are used to this now, and I don't mind at all – it's the least I can do, so we see that everyone gets what they are looking for and then we slip off back to the tour bus, where we start our journey across to my home town of Liverpool. Even thinking about playing in Liverpool makes me apprehensive. What if it doesn't go as well as tonight did? I get butterflies thinking about all the familiar sounds, faces and places that come with a home-town gig, and I don't think I'm going to sleep very well tonight, as so many things are going through my mind at the idea of playing such an iconic venue in the city I love so much.

As the tour bus takes us across from Manchester to Liverpool late that night, we pass some time playing cards, which, I have to admit, can get very competitive from time to time, but it's all very open and anyone can be a winner. Everyone is pretty good at the game of choice, which is Twenty-five, and although I do love winning, like the next man, I wouldn't say I'm an overly bad loser either, so it's all a bit of healthy fun and a nice way to relax and come down after a gig. Some of the lads wind me up about cheating, but all I can say is that I sometimes see the other players' cards by accident, and that's hardly my fault, is it?

I head to bed to catch up on *Hired Gun* on Netflix, a

documentary about famous musicians who are hired in to some of the world's biggest bands, like Billy Joel's band, Elton John's band, and how they fit in with life on the road. It's very interesting and, again, it's a nice way to unwind. I watched *Peaky Blinders* on the last tour, which I really enjoyed, and it's something to chat about to the others, who may be following it. We all seem to love a bit of Netflix to keep our minds occupied as we move around the country.

I fall asleep eventually and when I wake up and look out the window of the tour bus the next morning I see we have arrived safely at the Philharmonic Hall in Liverpool. I'm instantly overcome with a wave of emotion and nostalgia. This place means so much to me. I first sang here when I was just eight years old with my primary school as part of our Christmas concert, and then again when I came third place in the *Teen Idol* competition at the age of thirteen. I've seen a lot of big acts here as well down the years, including The Dubliners and Daniel O'Donnell, so it's sometimes hard to believe that the name on the bill tonight is my own.

Gareth, Barney and I head out to get some food and we call in to the Liffey Bar, where I used to play some of my very first pub gigs. Again, a flood of memories comes spilling out the moment I walk in the door – the smells, sights and sounds take me right back. This is where I saw and heard Nicky James when I was a young teenager, and this is where I knew, just from watching him, that I wanted to be able to have a crowd react to my music like he did. The bar has changed hands now, and I chat to the new management and let them know that we'll be back tonight after the gig with some friends and family, then we head back to the Philharmonic for the soundcheck, where the band and crew are ready to get started.

I step up on to the stage in the Philharmonic and, to my

surprise, it's not as big as I remembered it to be, but then that's the same as most places from your childhood; whether it's a school hall or a community centre, it all seems so much bigger through the eyes of a child. Years ago, I stood here scared stiff, just me and a microphone, and now it feels a lot more comfortable, but maybe that's because the stage is filled with the band and all our set and sound equipment, not to mention the bulk of the piano and the star cloth that lights up behind me – it's a whole lot cosier than I remember!

I start to feel the excitement bubbling as we run through a few songs on the soundcheck – it really is going to be a special night, and I've invited quite a few people – thirty-three, to be exact – including friends and extended family. My former accordion teacher, Geraldine Lynch, will be in the audience, as will some of the Comhaltas from Liverpool, and even some friends who used to see me gigging and who didn't really get the music I was into, plus Grumps, of course, and Mum and Dad, who I can't wait to see again after the show.

I don't have to wait that long, though, as during the sound-check Grumps makes his grand arrival.

'What time am I on?' he shouts up to me, and I know exactly what he is getting at.

'Oh, great, do you want to sing tonight, Grumps?' I ask him.

'No, no,' he replies. 'I wouldn't get up to sing unless I was asked properly.'

I roll my eyes and smile. It's an old, familiar routine.

'Would you like to join me on stage tonight for a song, please, Grumps?' I ask him politely.

He doesn't have to answer. I take all of that as a yes . . .

When the lights go up and I hear an audience reaction at any gig, I always kind of know what to expect from the rest of the gig, and the moment I hear the crowd roar in Liverpool I know that we're all in for a very, very good night. Around three rows of people stand up and sing along during the very first song, and it seems like the others are just raring to go, so we set off the way we mean to carry on and it feels amazing.

When the time is right, Barney goes into the audience and gives Grumps the nod to come and make his way up on to the stage for his grand appearance, and when the audience see him, they erupt and cheer and applaud. At eighty-four years old, Grumps looks as dapper as he did twenty, even thirty years ago. and the band don't even have to ask what he's going to sing, as they know it from before.

He sings 'Are You Lonesome Tonight?', adding in his old favourite 'Are your knickers too tight?' line, and I watch on in such awe and pride, thinking that, if I can look and act like that when I'm eighty-four, I'll be more than happy.

Grumps goes back to his seat, and the electric atmosphere keeps up for the rest of the show.

Two hours or so later, the gig ends with a standing ovation and I'm over the moon with how much the audience seem to have enjoyed it. I'm never completely happy with any gig, I'm always finding some little thing that could or should be tweaked, but this one was a stormer, and I know by the smiles on everyone's faces and the noisy reception we are getting that it was great, with Grumps perhaps stealing the show, as he always does!

I'm surprised and pleased to bump into a few of my old schoolfriends when we get to the Liffey Bar afterwards, and they tell me that they'd heard me on Radio 2 and also watched me and Nan on *The One Show*, which is surreal to me, to think that people outside of Ireland are now watching and listening in to the mainstream media coverage I'm starting to get this side of the Irish Sea. A lot of them do follow me on social media, so they know what's going on with my music, but it's very special to bump into them in person and to hear that they'd really enjoyed the show. The Liffey is packed with about three hundred people, and we're after a bit of live music so we head down to Mathew Street, where the famous Cavern Club, which showcases the legacy of The Beatles is, and we're delighted to see that Eric's Bar on the same street is buzzing with a live three-piece rock band. Perfect! We stay there till the early hours and end up in a casino at around 3.30 a.m., where I play about seven games and lose £60, which I'm gutted about. Realizing the time and that we'd really need to be getting back to the tour bus, I put a cheeky tenner on number thirty-six, and it comes in, winning me a cool £360, so it's McDonald's on me, bacon-and-egg McMuffins all round, and we enjoy them immensely when we get back on the bus around 5 a.m. and set off north on the two-hour journey to our next destination.

I wake up in Carlisle in the north of England around lunchtime, which is late for me to sleep in to, but I'm wrecked after a very late and eventful night in my home town.

Tonight is our fourth time selling out the Sands Centre here, and I'm excited to play it, even though I'm totally exhausted, so I nip inside to take a look around, upload some pics to social media and then grab a quick café lunch before it's time to do the soundcheck. I don't like to eat much before I sing, but I can't resist a small curry to give me some much-needed soakage.

Carlisle lives up to my expectations, as always, and the audience jump to their feet when we perform 'The Town I Loved So Well', even though I've had to leave out a few of the high notes as my voice is a bit sore and I'm not able to hit the notes without hurting my throat or straining my vocal chords. The audience seemed to really love it and, after the show, I spend at least an hour at the meet-and-greet before ordering a pizza (the only place open!) and crawl into my bunk before midnight, totally wrecked from an amazing weekend, as the bus drives us back to Liverpool, where we'll catch the first flight in the morning home to Belfast. That's one leg of the tour done. It's time to rest for a few days, and then we get to do it all over again.

Second Leg of the UK
Livin' the Dream Tour
(Thursday, 1 February–Monday, 5 February 2018)

After a few days of down time, which was spent at home in Enniskillen, with a few visits to the gym and a lot of Netflix, before we know it, it's Thursday again, and the alarm goes off once more at 5 a.m. to alert me that it's time to lift my case and make my way to the airport. This time, we're flying into Liverpool and making our way to Telford, a large town in Shropshire which is about thirty miles to the north-west of Birmingham. We catch a quick snooze on the bus, as usual, once we find our bunks and, when we get to Telford, it's time to check out the local Co-op, where we'll stock up on snacks and a few beers that will see us through to Monday – at least, that's the plan, anyway!

Nan arrives at lunchtime with her friends Barney and Carol, who make their way to front of house to set up the merchandise, and when soundcheck time comes we go over the acoustic set again as it's still quite new to us and we really want to rehearse it as much as we can. We make the call for Carl to bring on the double bass for the song 'King of the Road', which works a treat and, as we work through the set, Evan and Barney seem to be having lots of fun testing out the smoke machine.

Our food of choice – or should I say, lack of choice? – this evening is a Turkish takeaway. We discuss cinema listings and catch up on what we've all got up to on our days off, which, in Barney and Gareth's case, means spending precious time with their kids. I love to hear what Abbie (Gareth's daughter) and Ruben (Barney's son) get up to, and I can see how it can be hard for them to leave them again so soon.

The audience in Telford is lively and fun, and another good gig goes by without any major incidents, thank goodness. As I make my way to the tour bus, I remind myself how lucky I am to do this and to meet so many new people along the way. We relax with a few gin and tonics with Nan and sit up probably a bit too late for our first night and, before we know it, it's time to face the music the next morning and do it all over again.

When we wake up we're at the services, in Dunstable, Bedfordshire, as the venue is gated and wasn't open during the night, but soon we are parked up and hooked up onsite and a few of us set off to find a supermarket for some hot food for breakfast. There are a few sore heads on the bus this morning, and the sausage sandwiches don't go to waste when they're brought back to some of the hungry team. We discuss the latest Netflix viewing, which includes *My Super Ex-girlfriend* and *Homeland*.

Gareth, who spends a lot of time on the phone, is in despair as his beloved mobile has gone missing, only to turn up a while later in a box of Special K. I wonder how it got there, of all places?

Sausage sandwiches done, we're set up for the next few hours and it's time to get the rig in and prepare for the evening ahead. While the lads load in, I spend some time pondering answers to a press interview in the *Irish Examiner* which is asking me for my favourite romantic songs. The piece is in advance of Valentine's Day and ties in nicely with the release of my new single, 'This Song is for You', which is just about to go out into the open for the first time, but it's hard to think of romantic songs so early in the morning.

During the soundcheck we find a trolley at the back of the

stage and, much to our amusement, Barney pushes me across as I strike a Superman pose and Gareth makes a video of it for social media. The things we do to pass the time when waiting for the soundcheck to begin! I do a run-through of 'This Song is for You' and sing Colin Raye's 'Little Rock' to warm up my voice, then it's grub time and we find an all-you-can-eat Chinese, which, after the night before, really hits the spot. When we get back to the venue the audience is already filtering in and I get a few second glances as we walk past and make our way to the stage door. It's almost showtime.

The Haley Sisters are back with us again, and I love listening to their set, as do the audience, it seems, going by their reaction, and when it's our turn to take to the stage, everyone is well warmed up and they sing and dance in the aisles, rising to their feet again when I sing 'The Town I Loved So Well'. Thankfully, my voice is much stronger now, with a few shows behind me, and I manage to hit those high notes again with ease.

We go back to the bus after the meet-and-greet to find that the heating has been accidentally left on all evening and upstairs is unbearably hot. There's no way we could breathe, never mind sleep, up there, so we open any doors and windows we can find, and I have to say, everyone is very patient as they wait to be able to get some rest.

Despite our very late night in Telford – or should I say, as we travelled from Telford to Dunstable on the bus? – a few of the usual suspects manage to squeeze in a few drinks in a local sports bar and then on the bus when we get back, and once again I get to bed way too late, falling asleep with my phone playing Mary Black's 'No Frontiers' on repeat, which I'm sure delighted my neighbours in the bunks beside me. Let's hope they are all deep sleepers! After more than a couple of beers I hear nothing, of course, but I don't think others were so fortunate. Sorry, guys!

Cardiff is bustling when we get there the next morning, and Nan sets off to explore the shops as we're right bang in the city centre, at the magnificent St David's Concert Hall. There's an international rugby game on and we can barely get through the throngs of people, who are very much in sporting mood, with every restaurant and pub packed to the throat with fans decked out in blue, and in Wales colours, which I'm told are red (I did say I don't follow sport at all!).

When we get back for the soundcheck, we have a bit of rearranging to do as Tom, our fiddle player, has had to fly home that morning for a family wedding, so the lads have to sort out who will take on the various melodies that Tom normally takes a lead in. We work on it until our sound engineer, James, gives us the thumbs-up that he's made all the necessary adjustments to allow for Tom's absence on each song.

St David's Concert Hall has the big game on upstairs so the foyer is already heaving with people who are making the most of their evening out, and it's exciting to absorb the party-like atmosphere. This is my first time playing in Cardiff and, so far, so good. I really like it, and it's nice to be right in the heart of the city, where there is lots to see and do within walking distance.

JP and I go over a few new songs in the dressing room and we run through the song 'Carrickfergus' ahead of our performance with Brian Kennedy, which will happen in a few weeks' time at the SSE Arena in Belfast. I can't believe I'm returning there again, as well as to the 3Arena, and while I know that tickets are selling well, it barely sinks in that I might get to fill both venues again for the second time in a row.

Barney puts flyers out on the seats in St David's to promote the autumn UK dates and I do a quick Facebook Live video to update fans on how the tour is going and remind them to request my new song, 'This Song is for You', in time for Valentine's Day. My brother, Jake, is doing really well on *Dancing with the Stars*, so I remind everyone to tune in this evening and give him and his dance partner, Karen, their vote. I'm asked in the Facebook Live questions when we'll be coming to Boston, and then another fan asks when we'll be coming back to Billingham, which I can't answer, as we've just returned from there the weekend before! Another request comes in for Jo-Ann from The Haley Sisters to do her Cilla Black and Rocky impressions, so I turn the camera on her and, after a bit of convincing, she obliges, which goes down a treat. Jo-Ann can act almost anything, and her impressions are becoming a big part of this tour.

A few of us head out into the dark of the evening and into the city's bright lights to find a place to eat, but we are turned away from the first three places as everywhere is absolutely packed with rugby fans. Maybe the hunger was making me a bit delusional, but I come out with a statement that baffles the lads, who look at me like I've really lost the plot.

'I didn't realize they wore kilts in Wales too,' I say to them as we march through a sea of blue-and-white jerseys, blue curly wigs, blue-and-white painted faces and all sorts of tartan.

The lads stop in surprise.

'Are you serious?'

'Yes, what?' I ask. 'Do they wear kilts in Wales too? I didn't know that.'

'They are *Scottish* rugby fans,' I'm told emphatically. 'Wales were playing Scotland today. How could you possibly not have copped that on?'

I told you I knew nothing about sport . . .

When we're onstage later the Cardiff crowd, heightened in spirit by their big win in the rugby (I made it my business after that statement to find out who won), welcome us to Cardiff in style, and a few songs in I'm feeling very confident and relaxed in this all-new venue. I look out into the sea of faces, wondering where they have all come from. I feel so honoured to be playing this beautiful theatre for the first time. I certainly hope it won't be the last.

'This is our very first time in Cardiff,' I say to the audience, to massive applause.

And at that the sound totally cuts out. Not a kick. It's totally gone.

I look up at the sound desk, where James and Derek are calmly adjusting buttons, but it turns out it was nothing they had done and there was nothing they could do to fix it – it was an in-house problem.

Without hesitation, as we wait to get back on track I pick up the accordion and JP and Matthew join me at the front of the stage with their acoustic guitars. Carl follows on double bass and we launch into an unplugged Irish tune called 'Maggie in the Wood' until the sound comes back on.

Soon we're back in action, and the show goes on, ending with a standing ovation, once again during 'The Town I Loved So Well', which keeps everyone on their feet until the end of the show.

Despite it being a new venue in a new town, I do recognize some familiar faces, which is always nice. I really appreciate the effort people go to to come to my shows.

We get back on the bus close to 11.30 p.m. and, although we had planned to paint the town red (or blue, if you're Scottish), it's a very quiet night on the Nathan Carter tour bus and we are all tucked up in our bunks nice and early. There'll be no Mary Black on repeat tonight, as I go out for the count as soon as my head hits the pillow. Maybe I should adapt a 'shush' policy for the tour bus?

On second thoughts, maybe not . . .

Birmingham is the final city this weekend and when we

wake up from our deep slumber, we find that our driver has got us there safely and we're parked right outside the New Alexandra Theatre, which is tonight's venue.

Nan, who as always is ten steps ahead of us all, has already been out exploring, and she arrives on to the bus with a bright yellow suitcase.

'I thought this would be nice for the Caribbean cruise,' she announces to anyone who will listen. I just nod and agree.

'Yes, Nan,' I tell her. 'Good call.'

JP and I make our way that afternoon with my accordion and his guitar to the BBC's West Midlands studios, where we'll be guests on *Bob Brolly's Irish Programme*. Bob, who is originally from Derry, is a well-established personality in the Midlands and has always been very good to us when we visit the city, so I'm looking forward to seeing him again. We order an Uber to take us there and watch in bewilderment as our driver goes past us without stopping. Eventually, we flag a taxi down, much to my relief, as my arms are aching from carrying the accordion for so long. He drops us off and we make our way up three escalators to get to the studios, and I'm very glad to be able to set the accordion down in the foyer, where we are greeted by Bob's producers, Bridget and Sue, who present me with a goody bag when we get to Bob's studio. This takes me by surprise but, when I open it, I realize the joke! When they booked me for the show, the team asked me if there was anything I'd like on arrival, and I rhymed off a few difficult rider items like blue M&Ms, champagne, a Maltesers egg, some Belgian chocolates, Kit Kats and some home-made '15's, which are an Irish type of marshmallow bun. They hadn't known how to make these buns, but googled it and made them especially – it really set the tone of the interview, where we play 'Beeswing' and 'Wagon Wheel'. Bob even brings in a few fans who he'd heard were in the vicinity, which adds to the relaxed and friendly atmosphere that always comes with being on Bob's show.

Back at the Alexandra Theatre, I meet with Derek to go over the set design and lighting plans for the arena shows. We're going to have a 'B-stage' and I'm afraid it might look a bit bland, but Derek, as always, has some great ideas as to how we can make it the way I'd like it to be. We did a smaller version of this before, in the marquee at Cork, which brought me closer physically to the fans and also allowed the band to come out front when doing solos, bringing them right into the heart of the show.

Later on, as we kick off the show, the Birmingham theatre is packed and the show is merry and lively, but the very moment I come off stage I can feel my mood dip at knowing that it's the last night of the weekend. I really do feel a little bit down, knowing that another weekend of amazing gigs is over, and the thought of going home to doing chores like washing, banking and going to the gym fills me with dread. I'm already looking forward to Wednesday, when we'll be back on the road and, although some of the team feel the same, most are looking forward to getting home to see their family.

It's home time again, and I say goodbye and thanks to everyone, but we're only breaking for a few days' rest before we'll set off once more to put our show on the road.

The *Sunday World* Country Music Awards/Third Leg of the UK *Livin' the Dream* Tour
(Monday, 5 February–Monday, 12 February 2018)

After only about two hours' sleep on the tour bus the night before from Birmingham and an early-morning flight to Belfast, to say I am absolutely shattered is an understatement. Thank goodness JP is able to drive the jeep home from Belfast to Enniskillen, as I've a very busy day ahead.

I jump into bed the minute I walk in through the door at home at 11 a.m., sleep till 1 p.m., get up and put a load of washing into the machine, go to town to the bank and then pick up Lisa McHugh, who is getting a lift with me to the *Sunday World* Country Music Awards in the Mullingar Park Hotel, which is just under a two-hour drive from home.

The *Sunday World* Country Music Awards is a very well-attended annual event, with about one thousand people there every year, all eager to see who will pick up awards for categories including Best Songwriter, Best Single, Best Newcomer and Best Album in the world of Irish country music. When we get there at around 5 p.m. we are told that people have been queuing up outside from 2 p.m., all hoping to get a glimpse of their favourite acts on the bill, who include Derek Ryan, Foster and Allen, Johnny McEvoy, Cliona Hagan and many more.

I'm surprised to hear that I'm up for two awards, and after

we get through our soundcheck we go for dinner with some of the RTÉ team, including Ryan Tubridy, and discuss this year's plans for *The Late Late Show Country Special*, then it's back into the function room for the awards ceremony. I'm genuinely shocked when I'm told that I've won an award for Best TV Show and also for Best Arena Show. To get acknowledgement for these two elements of my career means a lot to me, and I really appreciate the industry nod from the *Sunday World*, plus, it's great to see some of my fellow *Sunday World* columnists, including Eddie Rowley and Father Brian D'Arcy.

After some quick hellos to some old friends and new, and a few photos with some of the fans and other acts including Una Healy, I leave for home at 9.30 p.m. and I'm in bed for 11.30 p.m., where I watch Sunday's episode of *Dancing with the Stars*. Jake is doing so well in the show and is proving to be quite a dancer, and when I'm finished watching his modern ballroom dance to the song 'Sign of the Times' by Harry Styles and see him awarded top marks from the judges, I am bursting with pride and emotion, almost crying with joy for him and so pleased that all his hard work is paying off. I've never seen him do anything like this, and I totally believe he has found something in addition to his music that he can be so, so proud of, as we are all so incredibly proud of him.

This weekend's set of tour dates take us to Chatham, Barnstaple, then two nights in Hayes, and it is business as usual after a much-needed rest, with all the gigs proving to be as enjoyable as the weekends before, though perhaps a bit quieter. We even manage to have some proper down time on a good old day off on the Friday!

I decide that it's time for some group bonding and that we

need to keep morale up, so we pool some suggestions as to what we could do that would keep us all together and be a bit of fun at the same time while we are parked up in Bristol.

Karting is suggested by a few, but it doesn't get the complete thumbs-up so in the end we agree on a day out at the bowling alley. The moment it is mentioned, you can feel the competitive streaks rise as everyone suddenly becomes a ten-pin champion – in their own head, at least. The afternoon is great craic and no one has to have the rails put up, which is a good sign. After a few decent rounds John Byrne is declared the winner, with Gareth graciously accepting his place at the bottom of the table.

We head off for pizza and more drinks after the bowling alley and, when we arrive back to the tour bus, we are met by Nan who, as usual, had done her own exploring of Bristol.

'Where've you been, Nan?' I ask her in dismay, glancing at the copious amount of bags she'd managed to drag around the town with her on her shopping spree.

'I've been to bingo,' she announces proudly. 'I've also been to Poundland, and I found a great bargain shop where I bought this pouffe for my friend back at home. What do you think?'

I look on with wide eyes as she presents the most horrendous pouffe covered with pictures of different types of dogs, but I have to pretend I like it. You just never know what Nan will turn up with next!

The third weekend of the tour brings some great news. I find out that my new single, 'This Song is for You', has made it to the top of the iTunes country chart. I come across it on Twitter, and it means so much to me as the single was only released on the Thursday, plus, it has leapfrogged two Taylor Swift songs and of course what makes it even more special is that it is a song I had written myself, along with Don Mescall.

Don travels in to meet me on the Saturday in Hayes and we spend the afternoon backstage churning out ideas for new songs. I really do enjoy locking heads with Don and we come away from the session happy, and I'm confident that we'll use some of the rock/country vibes we've come up with.

The Gertrude Byrne Thirtieth Anniversary Spectacular Caribbean Cruise
(Saturday, 17–Saturday, 24 February 2018)

Ship ahoy! It's time to sail the seas and get some longed-for sun in our bones! After weekend upon weekend on a fairly cramped (and sometimes smelly) tour bus, we are all very excited to be stretching our sea legs, and jetting off to the USA, to Florida, where we will stay for two days before embarking on the Gertrude Byrne Thirtieth Anniversary Spectacular Cruise. It will feature a host of Ireland's top entertainers onboard the prestigious MS *Nieuw Amsterdam*. The itinerary includes stops in Grand Turk, the Turks and Caicos Islands, Charlotte Amalie in the Virgin Islands, St Thomas, Phillipsburg in St Maarten, Half Moon Cay and the Bahamas.

It's a tough old life, but somebody's gotta do it!

Joining me on the line-up of the cruise, which is the world's only full-ship Irish charter cruise, are Engelbert Humperdinck, Charlie Pride and a host of Irish country stars, including my old friends The Benn Sisters, Jimmy Buckley, Mick Flavin and many more – but most importantly, I'm joined by the two people who took me on my very first cruise (just don't mention the price back then) and that is, of course, Nan and Grumps.

Grumps, who was thirty years at sea in his job as a purser, absolutely loves ships, so the excitement is very real when we land in Florida and meet up with Gareth and his fiancée, Emma, and John Pettifer and his girlfriend, Val, who I've known for a long time, as she used to work with Enjoy Travel. In fact, I credit myself very much in playing Cupid when it came to JP and Val's relationship as, three years ago, when I was arranging a dinner party, I invited Val along, knowing in the back of my mind that if she and John ever met they just might hit it off, as they have very similar personalities. Val is from Aughrim in County Galway, but she made the journey up for the dinner and, afterwards, when we went back to Lisa's house, the two kept talking and the rest is history!

In Florida, I get the chance to meet up with an old schoolfriend of mine, Anthony Barton, who is doing my other dream job out there as captain of a private yachting company. I'm also delighted to see that Vicky Kenny, a friend I've known for over five years, is also singing on the cruise.

We enjoy a few drinks in a bar in Florida as we wait to board the ship and I share a pic on social media of a barmaid kissing me on the cheek, not realizing the stir it would cause – it even made the *Daily Mail*, which was crazy, but I suppose the look of shock on my face was quite a picture!

As the ship's leaving party kicks off in true style, I can't help but reminisce about the Mediterranean cruise with Nan and Grumps, which was about twelve years ago now, when I was squeezed on to the bill at the last minute, due to some clever negotiating by Nan. Now, here I am, headlining a Caribbean cruise with big names like Engelbert and Charley, who my Nan absolutely adores. I'm so thrilled that Nan and Grumps are here to share this time with me, and I can't help but smile every time I look at them enjoying themselves so much as they sing and dance along to the entertainers who greet us as we make our way on to the magnificent ship. They really are the sweetest couple, and I love making as many memories as I can with them, especially as they gave me so many beautiful memories throughout my childhood.

Our shows on the ship take place over the next few days in a grand nine-hundred-seater theatre. I estimate that 90 per cent of the audience have never heard of me, so it's both exciting and nerve-wracking to be on this bill, but I give it my best shot and, to my delight, I have so many people, both fellow entertainers and the paying public, come up to me afterwards to compliment me on our show.

James and Derek work exceptionally hard on production, and the band all look like they are loving it – after all, there's nothing like some Caribbean sunshine to put a smile on your face! We work a total of two and a half hours over the course of the cruise, and the rest of the time is spent exploring the islands, going to casinos, lapping up the sun, drinking cocktails and hanging out in the hot tub. It's such hard work it almost reminds me of those labouring days out on the building site!

Apart from the gigs, which are a superb experience, one of the highlights of the cruise for me is when we get to visit Jimmy Buffett's bar, Margaritaville, which is on Grand Turk island. The bar is of course named after the song of the same name which was a huge hit in 1977. In it he sings about a laid-back lifestyle in a sunny climate, and I really could get used to this – turquoise seas, colourful cocktails and not a care in the world! It's all very commercialized, but so picturesque, and we all lap up every moment of the time we spend there, drinking in the atmosphere and the cocktails!

Every night on the ship there's a great sing-song in the piano bar, where I sing and jam with The High Kings, Dominic Kirwan, Jimmy Buckley and anyone else who wants to do their party piece, so the cruise definitely proves to be a holiday to remember.

Nan and Grumps have an absolute ball, apart from when, on the last day, Grumps has to be treated for dehydration as he hadn't drunk enough water with his whiskey! Thank goodness he was okay and thank goodness, also, for travel insurance!

We set off for home fully refreshed and full of smiles and memories, plus, on a professional level, I had gained a whole new audience, many of whom I hope will come back and see me and the band when we return to America later in the year.

After the cruise, JP and I fly into Nashville for a three-day recording session at Omni Studios, where we lay down some tracks for my next album. The first day is spent preparing keys and finalizing songs, while the following two days will be spent recording with some of Nashville's finest session musicians.

We check out some of the usual Nashville hotspots, finding some honky-tonk music, and we call into the very famous Tootsie's bar, but it's early to bed. I have two twelve-hour recording sessions the next day, and I have to be on the ball as I'll be working with guys who have played with Tim McGraw, Alan Jackson and Randy Travis – all of whom I grew up listening to on those WMZQ tapes I used to be sent from my uncle Van's family in Washington DC.

The session leader is called Jamie Mitchell, and we easily get through sixteen songs in total, including seven original songs for the new album which will be released this summer. Recording in Nashville is so productive and quick – these musicians are so pristine and they do this every day. Jamie is a guitar player who worked with Alison Krauss and is one of the finest I've ever seen, so it's really cool to have him on the album, and JP, who arranged the music for the album and who of course plays guitar in our band, is also blown away by his talent.

As well as working long and heavy but very productive days, JP and I do manage to treat ourselves to some nice dinners, and we enjoy meeting up with Ralph Murphy, the songwriter who I'd written some songs for this album with.

With a successful few days under our belt, we're looking forward to making our way home, where we're booked to play in Adare Manor in County Limerick at a private function the following night, but Storm Emma has other ideas, as she has grounded Dublin airport to a standstill and our flight is delayed. Just as panic really begins to set in, we're boarded for our first flight to Chicago, then on to Dublin, making it just in time – but our drama isn't over just yet as there are absolutely no taxis available to take us to City North, where my jeep is parked. We try Uber, but no joy. The entire city is on lockdown and the streets are empty, we're told. Luckily, we bump into a driver who is waiting for someone and he offers to take us to City North – it's touch and go as he makes his way to where we parked the jeep and, just when we are about to exhale with relief, we get a phone call to say the gig has been cancelled, due to the ferocious weather.

So with nothing else for it, we take our time and make our way home to Enniskillen, where I arrive just in time to get cosy and put my feet up to do what most of the country seems to be doing, as the weather is too bad to go out anywhere.

I switch on *The Late Late Show* and watch in awe as Ryan Tubridy presents for the first time to an almost empty studio. The weather has forced them to cancel the usual live studio audience for health-and-safety reasons. Most of the guests have cancelled also, which means that my good friend Cliona Hagan, who is on to provide some music, gets to take a seat in the interviewee's chair and chat to Ryan, and she even gets to sing a second song as most of the nation tunes in on one of the stormiest nights of the year so far. Storm Emma was certainly working in Cliona's favour, and it couldn't have happened to a nicer person!

Blackpool Weekend
(Friday, 9 March–Sunday, 11 March 2018)

It may be a long way from Nashville and the balmy Bahamas to blustery Blackpool, but that isn't going to dampen our spirits, as I'm very excited that, after a whole lot of planning, this big weekend is finally here.

It's my first time to headline my own Blackpool weekend, having been a guest on a few others before, and we've put so much work into preparing for it, so my hopes are high that it's going to be a real success and an enjoyable weekend for all the Irish, Scottish and English people who have made their way to the Hilton Hotel to join me and my guests over three days of dancing and song.

I fly into Liverpool on the Thursday afternoon and spend some time with my parents before setting off early in the morning in Dad's car north to Blackpool, stopping off when we get there for some lunch, which takes for ever. I begin to panic because I'm due to record a radio interview at the Hilton Hotel and my chicken Caesar salad takes ages to arrive! As well as the time constraints, I'm absolutely starving, and after a whole forty-five-minute wait we really do question whether they've forgotten about us. As it turns out, it wasn't the salad at all that was holding things up, but the goat's cheese tart that Mum had ordered, so when Dad and I explain we are in a hurry, they serve up mine, and we have to leave Mum to it for a few minutes while Dad drops me off at the Hilton Hotel, just in time to get in front of the mic and go live on the radio.

I'm delighted to see that the team from Enjoy Travel have

everything running like clockwork, as always, with a registration table set up in the hotel foyer, and they issue everyone who has booked in for the weekend with a wristband so that they can gain entrance to all of the entertainment we've planned for them. Just beside his table, Nan does what only Nan does best on the merchandise stall, with her friend Carol, and Carol's husband, Barney, and Denise, who runs my fan club, gives out goody bags, which include a bar of tequila-flavoured Blackpool rock, which, you guessed it, Nan had sourced on one of her research trips. She never fails to impress me with her planning and eye for detail!

It's a busy foyer at the Hilton as fans of all ages begin to arrive, and the place oozes excitement, with many people spotting others they know. It's so nice to see young families turn up to enjoy the weekend with their children, as well as older folk, who are just as keen to get the party started!

Nicky James entertains in the afternoon in the hotel bar, and the evening show is opened by another good friend, Stuart Moyles, before we take to the stage for our Friday-night concert. It's great to have Mum and Dad in the audience, and I sing a song for them, as well as for my cousin Savannah, who is celebrating her twentieth birthday. It's such a nice feeling to know that my family is there to support me, and I'm really delighted to see my aunt Siobhan, her husband, Van, and kids Savannah, Molly and Liam, plus, Savannah's boyfriend, Terry. My great-uncle, Nan's brother Simon O'Neill, is there too, with his wife, Muriel, and the next day my aunt Oona will arrive with her husband, Steve, so lots of close relatives are here to give moral support.

We finish off our Friday night with a nosey around some of the bars in Blackpool, and the next morning I enjoy a late breakfast in my room before welcoming my Saturday guests, Philomena Begley, Cliona Hagan and her manager, Aidan

Quinn, to the hotel for a few snacks and a glass of wine as jiving lessons take place in the function room downstairs.

I spend some time mingling with fans later in the afternoon and, as it's my dear Nan's birthday, she is, as I thought she would be, very busy accepting millions of presents and cards from fans when I go to give her a card and pressie on the merchandise stall.

I decide to take a break from the hotel to seek out some Chinese food before tonight's show, which is cabaret in style this time, with round tables filling up the function-room floor. Tonight's show is a bit more relaxed than last night's seated concert, and Nan is brought to the stage to receive a birthday cake and enjoy her moment as hundreds of people sing 'Happy Birthday' to her, Blackpool style. Afterwards in the bar we enjoy some dancing ourselves and I get to catch up with lots of familiar faces who I've come to know down the years, including the Hester twins, Brendan and Kieran, who are champion Irish dancers, and lots of fans and friends from Donegal, Derry and South Armagh. We find a residents' bar, then a piano, and then it's back to my room on the top floor for some late-night music and drinks. Thank goodness I don't have to put a mattress up against the door on this occasion to block out the sound, as I'd say most of the people in the hotel are partying the night away also!

Sunday afternoon begins with a family-friendly dance in the same big function room and then it's time to say goodbye to fans and family members, all of whom are fully charged with adrenaline and full of beans after an absolutely brilliant weekend.

I travel up to Manchester with JP and we catch a flight to Dublin, where we arrive just in time to catch some of the Country 2 Country Festival, which features Tim McGraw (who collapsed on stage from dehydration), his wife, Faith

Hill, and out on the *Sunday World* stage is our very good friend Lisa McHugh, who we cheer on with pride as she entertains the audience.

The night is young when the concert is over, and we finish it off in Lillie's Bordello, where I take to the piano and sing a few songs. The next day, while still in Dublin, I am interviewed on the Ray D'Arcy show on RTÉ where I give possibly one of the hoarsest interviews I've ever done.

I blame you, Blackpool, and all your boldness! I have officially lost my voice!

Fourth leg of the UK *Livin'*
the Dream tour and St Patrick's Day
at the London Palladium
(Thursday, 15 March–Monday, 19 March)

Sandwiched between gigs in Nottingham and Christchurch on Thursday and Friday and Sunday night in Clacton-on-Sea is a night that will always stand out for me as one of the highlights of my career.

Ten years ago, I was playing three pubs in one day around Liverpool to mark St Patrick's Day and now, here I am, looking out of the tour bus at giant lit-up displays featuring my name and photograph next to the name of none other than the London Palladium for their St Patrick's Night concert.

Ireland has won the rugby (yes, I've done my sports homework this time) and the lads in the band are on massive form. We discuss in wonder the whirlwind of the last few months, which has brought us to so many amazing places and taken me to so many peaks in my career. Now, I'm in London, about to take the stage in front of an audience who are decked out in green and who seem just as excited as we all are to be there.

The London Palladium holds 2,200 people and they all make sure their voices are heard when our support act, All Folk'd Up, who I've loved for many years, open the show. All Folk'd Up, who are one of the best traditional/Celtic rock acts out there right now, have been gigging all week in Cheltenham, so they are already on a high and can't wait to rock the Palladium. The band receives a roaring response, which is very well deserved, and by the time we start up after them the entire audience is on their feet!

We throw in a few extra Irish songs to add to the atmosphere, such as 'Homes of Donegal' and 'Summer in Dublin' and, as the London Palladium doesn't allow for meet-and-greets in the venue itself, I can't help but squeeze in a thirty-minute slot for fans to come and say hello and have a picture taken after the show out by the tour bus.

After playing the Palladium on my birthday the year before, I thought I knew what to expect from this night, but nothing could have prepared me for the reaction we got and the whole buzz in the room from start to finish. It was magical, and it made me very proud to be in such an iconic venue, surrounded by people who were enjoying themselves so much, and all in a celebratory way of all things Irish.

We round off the night at an Irish Gala Ball at a nearby hotel, which we were all invited to, and despite the price of drink almost knocking us over in shock, we toast a fantastic night as excitement brews for the week ahead.

It's the big one we've all been waiting for. We're going back to take on the arenas in Ireland.

The Irish Arena Gigs – 3 Arena, Dublin and SSE Arena, Belfast
(Monday, 19–Saturday, 24 March 2018)

Monday morning brings me to EJ Menswear in Sligo, where I pick up a pale blue suit I'd decided upon a while ago to wear on the biggest stages I'd play in 2018 – the 3 Arena in Dublin and the SSE Arena in Belfast.

Once again, just like the year before, we put our money where our mouth was and took a gamble that enough people in two of Ireland's most prominent cities would come out and see us again in a production that we'd all put our heart and soul into preparing for.

The guest list was drawn up well in advance, with many friends who had helped me get this far coming along to one of the two gigs. My parents travelled over from Liverpool, bringing ten friends with them, and even Nan would be able to sit back and relax in the audience, as arena staff were to take over merchandising. (I'm not too sure she was too impressed, mind you, as she couldn't get talking to all her buddies, who she knew would be there!)

Having settled on my outfit of choice, it's time for rehearsals, which, this time, are going to take place in a rehearsal space in Lucan, just outside Dublin city. We spend a full day on production, going over lighting and sound and special effects and, just to keep us on our toes, the pyrotechnics decide not to work on the trial, and this means that we can't test them again – the next time they are operated will be at the gigs for real at the weekend.

We've adjusted the set to suit each venue and I've learned a beautiful song called 'Belfast', which was recorded by a band called Barnbrack. I'll be singing this alone, accompanying myself on piano, and I hope the audience find it as poignant to listen to as I do to perform. In Belfast, I'll be joined by two special guests – my good friend Lisa McHugh, who will sing the John Cougar classic 'Hurt So Good' with me, and the highly renowned Brian Kennedy, who will share the stage with me for a haunting rendition of 'Carrickfergus'. In Dublin I'll be welcoming Mary Black as part of the show, and we've added in that good old Bagatelle sing-along favourite, 'Summer in Dublin'.

During the rehearsals in Lucan I take a quick break to shoot a VT with Jake and his dance partner, Karen, who have, remarkably, made it to the final of *Dancing with the Stars*, which will be broadcast live on television the Sunday after our gig in Belfast. I'm immensely proud of Jake, should he win the grand final prize or not, and I honestly don't know how our parents are going to contain themselves throughout the weekend between the two arena gigs and then the big final to look forward to on Sunday. What a weekend for the Carter family!

The week rolls on and I line up several promotional interviews, including one on the *Lynette Fay Show* on Radio Ulster, which I always enjoy. Before I know it, Friday is here and it's time to face the music officially – it's absolutely crazy, and sometimes so hard to take in that I am here doing this again. I can't believe that people have gone and bought tickets and travelled from all corners of Ireland to hear me and the band in such a huge space and on such a massive stage, when I spent so many years in awe of many international acts and longed to have that level of success.

Now, here I am doing it for real.

Both shows are truly magical, and we go through a range of emotions – from watching on with pride as Jake and his band open the show, followed by Hayseed Dixie, to my grandparents slow-dancing as I sing 'Good Morning, Beautiful'. I point out little Padraig in Belfast, whose dad shared his version of 'Wagon Wheel' so that I could see it on Facebook, we do a hell of a Mexican wave, which always takes my breath away, and in Belfast my idea of a quick change into a kilt for a selection of Scottish-themed songs doesn't exactly go according to plan and I almost suffer a very embarrassing wardrobe malfunction which makes me laugh and feel a bit scared at the same time!

The Dublin audience dance until they almost drop, and when I sing The Dubliners' 'Rare Auld Times', they sing the chorus three times on their own. I just stand there with goose bumps, wondering how on earth I got so lucky.

We finish each night of the arena gigs on an ultimate high with our own rendition of 'Live and Let Die', an idea that JP brought to the table, having seen it done by Paul McCartney, and as the pyrotechnics go off, smothering the stage and the audience with masses of red confetti, I take a deep breath and close my eyes, absorbing every single second of this moment that I'd always dreamed of.

I think back to that first CD I made and how my beloved Nan drove through the night to have it pressed so that I could make that first cruise, and how she almost broke the bank (and almost gave Grumps a heart attack!) by blowing the budget on the big fancy room.

I think back to the fleadhs and the dodgy caravans and the moment of joy when I won my All Ireland title for singing.

I think of leaving Liverpool when I was such a young lad, full of hopes and dreams, knowing no one, and not having a clue what was going to be round the next corner or if things were going to go my way.

I think back to the days when I played those almost empty venues in Ireland, giving people back their money if there weren't enough punters in to pay the band.

I look down at my parents and my grandparents in the audience and I well up, thinking of their support, their belief, and of people like John Farry and my amazing band, who work so hard to enable me, Nathan Carter, to do what I do to the very best of my ability.

I truly believe that we have to guide our own destiny in life.

You have to be the one who decides where it is you want to go and how it is you are going to get there. In my job, the buck stops with me, and it always has and always will. If I want to be a success, I'm going to work my ass off to make that happen and, so far, I know that, every step of the way, I've worked really, really hard.

My dad always told me that, if you believe in something enough and if you work hard enough in life, you'll get it, and I've always kept those words in the back of my mind – thanks, Dad! As I keep doing what I love to do so much, I don't think I'll ever lose that drive to be the very best I can. It's in me, it's who I am and it's how I've been brought up by the best parents and the strongest, most encouraging family and peers.

The past twenty-seven years have been amazing for me, Nathan Carter.

The future is looking even better. But, for now, it's time once more to get back on the road and keep doing what I know I do best.

From the Fans

A huge thank-you to all the fans who sent in their stories for the book. We had hundreds of fantastic stories and enjoyed reading every single one of them. These are just some of our favourites:

Nathan Carter is truly a delightful individual and singer. My sister and I went to two of his US concerts last year and met him each time. He remembered us and was so kind . . . and he smelled great!

While it's super-special to see how much Nathan cares about his fans (and interacts with us via social media), his real talent is in his live show! Not only is he a stellar show-man, he is cross generational – teens, adults and elderly, all were rocking the venues we attended!

Nathan also seems super-supportive of his band, which I congratulated him on during both his meet-and-greets I attended. They seem like a stellar group of guys who just happen to support one of the most talented singers of this century!

We currently have tickets to every Branson, MO, show for November 2018! We are *soo* looking forward to seeing Nathan perform again.

– Brandy W. Eckis, Branson, Missouri

I have only ever had the good luck to see Nathan when he has come to Scotland, as I live in chronic pain through a spinal injury, which led to six spinal surgeries. I now am in a wheel-chair. When you are in chronic pain, you look for something to relax you and ease your pain, and I find listening to Nathan's music and watching his DVDs gives me that distraction. I have met Nathan after his shows in Perth and Dundee and, although I can feel embarrassed being in a wheelchair, Nathan has never made me feel like he doesn't have time for me and even asks my mum how she is. Nathan has brought something new and refreshing to the music industry and I believe he was brought up with good family roots and this made a big difference. He has many more good times ahead.

– Teresa Burns, Auchterarder, Scotland

Nearly eight years ago I first went to see Nathan in the Greenhills Hotel in Limerick. There were just over twenty people at it! Ever since then I have followed Nathan all over Ireland and England.

About seven years ago my friends for my birthday bought me a blow-up doll with Nathan's face on it and, since then, the doll has travelled all over with us. Needless to say, my husband (my boyfriend at the time) was a little concerned Nathan's face was on it, not his! Roll on to my hen party in 2016, and while most hens have the bride's future husband's face everywhere, on mine it was Nathan's face that was everywhere!

– Laura McCarthy, Limerick

I first met Nathan in Loughrea Spa Hotel in Galway back in 2014 when I was having a rough time, as I had ended a relationship and lost my dad a few years before that. Nathan's music opened a new chapter in my life and helped me beat depression. After the Loughrea gig I went and bought all his old albums, first, to listen to the songs I heard at the gig. From 2015 on, Nathan changed my life. I was able to come off my antidepressants and had a new lease of life. When

Nathan took his show to the UK I was so mad at myself, as I had a fear of flying, but I booked tickets to see him at George's Hall in Bristol and then the London Palladium and, with the help of reading a book on the plane to distract me, I made the journey. Yes, Nathan and his music made me overcome my fear of flying! Once I'd started flying to the UK, I couldn't stop and, since then, I've been to Liverpool, Newcastle-on-Tyne, Manchester, Edinburgh, Aberdeen, Glenrothes, Glasgow, and best-place-ever Benalmádena two years in a row for his Carter on the Costa. Nathan changed my life with his music therapy, he helped me grow stronger and bigger in life. I've made numerous new friends for life through Nathan. All I have to say is thanks so much, Nathan for the love of your music, your dedication and hard work. My mum, Margaret, my daughters, Saoirse and Sarah, and I all think you're amazing.

– Claire McCormack, County Galway

The date 14 October 2013 will forever hold a special place in my heart. I honestly believe I will remember it for ever. It was the date of my very first Nathan Carter concert. I had heard and read great reports about this new country singer on the scene, but I was itching to see for myself. I remember entering through the door to take my seat and was hardly able to sit down, with the sheer excitement of the concert that lay ahead of us. Nathan came on and sang his heart out. It was the best night, I felt, of my whole life and from that night on I became an avid fan. I went home on a high, already making plans in my head for his next concert. I couldn't believe how talented he was and how I had never heard of him until now. Sadly, however, my world came crashing down around me two weeks later, as I received devastating news, the news that every woman dreads receiving. I was diagnosed with breast cancer. I can, however, say with absolute confidence that it was Nathan and his wonderful music that got me through my illness. I listened to a beautiful song he sang the first night I went to his concert called 'Lay Down beside Me'. Maybe it was his beautiful voice or the way he sang those words, but that sound inspired me and helped me through my worst battle. It helped me to not give up hope that I would get through my illness. My daughter entered my name into a competition on social media, which I won, with the prize being a meet-and-greet with Nathan. Finally, I was going to meet this wonderful man whose music helped me in ways he would never know. It was truly a dream come true for me. I was so grateful to be given such an opportunity. Nathan was an absolute gentleman and meeting him is something I will cherish for ever. I am now in remission and have decided to live my life the very best way that I can, which includes plenty more Nathan Carter shows. I have been to fifteen of his shows since that very first night and each one is better than the previous one. To me, Nathan is without a shadow of a doubt the best country singer out there. Nobody else comes close.

– Helen Guiry, Nire Valley, County Waterford

I first heard of Nathan last year when he did a special on PBS here in the States. I'm sorry to say I only caught the last thirty minutes of the show, but that was enough to get me hooked on his music!! I searched YouTube, and found his music and style just absolutely wonderful! I now have all of his CDs and DVDs and never tire of listening to or watching them. I was thrilled when I heard he was coming to America and Rochester was his first stop. I got front-row tickets! I had no idea until that night that I would be meeting him before the show. I'd never met a star before and when he came out I acted like a star-struck teenager, which I'm far from, at sixty-one years old! I got my picture taken with him and Chloe, and his autograph as well. The show was fantastic and I decided to see him at another of his shows in Boston, Massachusetts. His music and songs have so much feeling and meaning in them. They get me through the forty-five-minute drive to and from work every day. Not really sure how to explain it, but listening to him sing just calms me more than any other singer, and I grew up listening to country music. He can take a song and make you feel like he is singing just for you. I look forward to seeing him again when he comes back to the States. Thank you, Nathan, for your music, your songs, your energy and compassion! You are truly a talented singer and performer!

– Paula Voorhees, Victor, New York

My lovely god-daughter, Jennifer Payne, is from Bandon, County Cork, and she has special needs. She is twenty years old and absolutely adores Nathan Carter.

Jennifer has Nathan's photo and his name on the wheels of her wheelchair. She has life-size cardboard cut-outs of him, every CD; every bit of merchandise that he has out, Jenn has it. She knows every song he has ever brought out and every time I speak to her on the phone I can hear Nathan in the background. She comes over to my house every Tuesday and we have a Nathan Carter concert for four hours.

We went to see Nathan in 3Arena last year. He was fantastic, but Jenn was disappointed as she didn't get to see him, but his nan, grandad, sister, aunt and some of the band members were staying in the same hotel as us. Nathan's nan is so nice to us and chats to Jenn at every concert we see her at. His grandad sang three beautiful songs to her. We met band members in the lift the following morning, which led to huge excitement, and ever since that day the bass player, Carl, has been so nice to Jenn.

But the most important and stand-out moment for me is when we met Nathan in the Marquee in Cork three years ago. To my surprise, my shy little moll Jennifer wrapped her arms around Nathan and asked him to marry her! He replied that it would happen in a few years and, ever since then, she always asks him where her ring is!

Jennifer adores Nathan and we as a family would like to thank him so much. He just doesn't realize what he does for people, especially for our girl Jennifer.

— Sandra Day, County Cork

Nathan is a very special guy to me. It's not easy being a single mum of three and it can be hard to get a night out, but the first time I heard Nathan sing 'Wagon Wheel' I thought I must get to one of his shows. A few weeks later, Nathan came to our GAA club in Magherafelt. There was a competition to win two tickets, so I entered it and I can remember that I was heading out the Saturday night and I wondered why I got so many notifications from friends, so I checked it out and I had won the tickets! The excitement was unreal. I did a wee dance around the kitchen! Since then I've gone to see Nathan as often as I can and I've met a great friend in Una Doherty, who I believe can claim to be Nathan's number-one fan, as she never misses a show. The energy and atmosphere at Nathan's concerts is something special and his music really touches my heart.

— Kelley Farmer, Magherafelt, County Derry

Being introduced to Nathan and his music has literally changed my life, and for that I will always be so grateful.

I was meant to go to my first concert on New Year's Eve 2015 but made excuses not to go, as at that stage I was over ten stone heavier than I am now and would rather sit in and not be seen, plus, going out had to be planned, like the type of seats there would be and whether I'd fit in them, and God forbid if I had to stand!!

Out of guilt I allowed myself to be dragged to my first concert in January 2016, and I got such a lift from Nathan's performance that for the time I was there I forgot everything and just got lost in the music. It left me with a feeling of wanting more. By the 3Arena concert in March 2016 I'd received a blast of energy – it literally hit me in the gut. It must have been a big blast of energy, as it was a very big gut! I nearly broke my friend's arm pulling at it, saying, 'Did you feel it? Did you feel it?'

I summoned the courage to queue for a picture and got to meet Nathan, and walking away from that first meet-and-greet, I turned around to my friend and said, 'Nathan has got rid of my brain fog, I can see the sun. I want my life back.'

It was the spark I needed to get myself out of the dark place I'd been in and to stop feeling sorry for myself. Within a couple of weeks I started a plan and I knew this time it would be different. I wanted it. I wanted life. I wanted to be able to stand at Nathan concerts and not have to hold on to the barrier to do so, and I wanted to go to Carter on the Costa and be able to jive.

By the time Carter on the Costa October 2016 came, I was seven stone lighter, and had started jive classes, a big thing for me, as before I couldn't get up off the sofa without using a crutch. So many things have happened since – I have made some great friends, my life has been totally transformed – all triggered off from that spark I received from Nathan.

My life has even changed in simple ways, like being able to help my mother and others in the time of the snow with

Storm Emma, being able to walk up and down our hill three times in the day to run errands. It wouldn't have been physically possible before — you wouldn't have got me outside of the door.

I thank Nathan for the music, the dancing but, most of all, for setting me free.

— Olivia Garcia, County Cavan

Nathan's music has helped me pull through a lot of dark times in my life. I love everything about country and folk music, especially the lyrics, which I can really relate to. I'm on a high dose of medication, but my nurse has told me to do what makes me happy, and that is listening to country music and going to concerts. Now my daughters are coming along too, and we're making so many good memories, while blocking out a lot of bad memories. I've even made new friends across Ireland, and I'm so grateful.

— Emma Back, Limerick

I travelled down from Belfast to Enniskillen, where my nannie and auntie live, to see Nathan Carter in concert in the Ardhowen Theatre on a chilly October night. It was the first time to see Nathan in concert and, most importantly, my nannie's first time at a concert ever. We all thought the concert was fabulous, and we queued up with the crowd for the meet-and-greet at the end to get my poster signed, which Nathan's lovely granny minded at the merchandise table. My nannie stood away from the crowd, as she doesn't like herself in pictures. As we were getting closer to getting our photo taken we noticed my nannie talking to a gentleman who we assumed she knew locally from Enniskillen. I called over to my nannie to get into a photo, which is where Nathan himself laughed and said, 'I must rescue your nannie from my granda.' Nathan then went over to my nannie and we got a photo of us all together. Perfect ending to a great night out.

– Ciara Lindsay, Belfast

My mum, Maureen, is from Tipperary. She has followed Nathan since the very beginning, and five years ago she took me along to my first Nathan Carter gig after I'd been listening to her for many years talking about him! As you know, Nathan was on tour in the UK for the first three months of 2017, so the only Irish date was 1 April in 3Arena. As somebody who goes to Nathan's shows on a regular basis, she said there was no way she could survive for a whole three months without seeing Nathan. So I asked her would she go to one of the UK gigs, thinking she would say no, as she has never been outside Ireland in her life. She has missed family weddings, funerals and parties because she refused to go on a boat or a plane. She said she would go to the Birmingham gig. I couldn't believe it – at seventy-one years of age she was leaving Ireland and going on a plane for the first time ever. We went to Birmingham and she loved the plane . . . we never said anything to Nathan about coming. His face was a total surprise when he spotted her in the audience that night, as he knew she had never been out of the country. The gig was excellent and when we met Nathan after the show he was asking her how was the flight and was delighted to see her.

That was 4 February 2017, a date that will stick in my mind for ever. Since then she has been to Carter on the Costa in Spain and two more of Nathan's shows in Manchester and Liverpool. She says she feels she is only living now all the things she has missed out on over the years. She has seen Nathan live over a hundred times and has been one of his most dedicated fans from day one. It's all down to Nathan that she has overcome her fear of flying, and nothing will hold her back now! Music does save the soul, even when you think there is no hope. Nathan has been a light in our lives and we just want to thank him for it.

– Sharon Lyons, Kilkenny

I've been running a radio show in Blackpool for over five years and Nathan was one of the first Irish stars I interviewed. Over the years I have interviewed Nathan many times and been to many shows, and he has become a friend.

In 2017 my wife and I separated and I became more or less a single dad. Nathan's music became a bond I share with my six-year-old son, Kirian, and Nathan has always made time to see him before shows, so much so that last Christmas Kirian asked Santa for an accordion so he could perform like Nathan. Nathan is such a genuine guy and a good friend with a big talent and a bigger heart. I wish you all the best, my friend and thank you.

– Tom Collins, Lytham, St Anne's

Since getting into Nathan's music I don't even know myself any more, and neither do a lot of other people! They say things to me like, 'Since we've been friends, I've never heard you talk as much, laugh as much or seen you smile as much as you do now.' To hear things like that means the world to me. For years I've suffered with severe anxiety and Nathan just helps me forget about that for a while. Whenever I'm upset, his music sorts me out, no matter what. I love the gigs so much I just come alive whenever I'm there. I call them 'my happy place'. I've been to see Nathan twelve times now in my two years of being a fan and met him eight times, and I can honestly say he is probably the nicest person I've ever met. He's just so approachable and takes so much interest in his fans and everything they want to say. We've had some funny times together too. He comes out with things like, 'I'll be all over Twitter later, Amy, will I?' and 'Will we get a selfie for Twitter?' I call myself his favourite Twitter torment lol! Thank you from the bottom of my heart for everything, Nathan.

– Amy Loughrey, Drogheda

I've followed Nathan from the very beginning and I always knew he would go right to the top. My mum and I follow him everywhere. She says he's her 'wee bit of therapy'. Two years ago, she had a heart operation and Nathan heard about it. He took the time to phone her and wish her well. To me, that's what makes him so special. He always goes that extra mile. I even have Nathan Carter tattoos!

– Judith Knipe, Cookstown

My dear friend Annie and I were kindred spirits. We had a friendship that blossomed from being introduced through a mutual friend into a friendship that was as strong as any married couple. We called each other 'my better half'.

On many occasions as we drove all over the country there would only be one voice playing on our journey, and that was, as Annie called him, 'my Nathan'. Annie was always looking for our next trip away to see the man himself in concert, and listening to his music became a form of therapy for both of us. From relationships ending, difficulties with work, and so on, no matter what we were going through, when we put Nathan's music on it took us away into our own wee world.

Annie and I really started to get the dancing bug.

From Santa Ponsa to Donegal, the trips to hear Nathan kept coming our way, and we became big fans. On the way to one concert we planned to stop off in the Lough Erne and Annie told me to pull in to the park where the boats were, as she wanted to have a look around. So as her ladyship had asked, I pulled the car in. Almost at a high pitch, Annie squealed, claiming she had just spotted Nathan. I laughed in disbelief but, before I could say anything more, she was gone to say hello. At first, I didn't believe her that it was him, but as I looked over, watching as she went towards this fella, who, like myself, was watching the ducks, as if he had a fear of birds like myself. I watched on as she stood for a few minutes and had this conversation with Nathan, but I couldn't move as I was afraid to get out of the car because of the hundreds of ducks. Then, with the two arms swinging and again a massive smile on her face, the bold Annie walked back over to the car. All I could see was her exaggerated facial expressions showing her extreme happiness at talking to Nathan.

In 2017 Nathan's music was to become even more poignant in our lives as in June of that year Annie had started to feel unwell. Annie was given the news that her cancer had come back and it was at a very severe stage. Within three hours we were on our way to St Luke's in Rathgar. As we travelled up the M3, just the three of us – Annie, 'her Nathan' and I, the journey seemed to flash every memory we had together and it was the hardest road we had ever travelled. Nathan's album *Stayin' Up All Night* was the CD we had chosen to listen to over the road to Cavan. As we just passed the toll I will always remember that song number eleven, 'Don't Know Lonely', came on. With both of us with sunglasses on, we held hands and, as much as I could, I tried to hold back the tears that were flooding my sunglasses from falling so Annie didn't see, as I had to be strong. We spent a week in St Luke's and, throughout that week, when it was just the two of us, Nathan was put on YouTube and his albums were listened to as we organized and planned what had to be done. Returning home was something that again made Annie feel happy, as she got to see her family and friends.

Deborah, a family friend who is involved in the country scene, knew how much Annie loved Nathan and, unknown to Annie, they had arranged for Nathan to come along to her house and to meet with her for that one-to-one she had always been talking about. It was a struggle for us all to try and keep this surprise from her, as she had asked me from the start to be by her side and to always tell her the truth, no matter how bad things were to get. Unfortunately, as the day was approaching Annie became unwell and we had to return to Cavan Hospital. As we were travelling over the road to the hospital, Annie said to me, 'Please, David, be honest . . . was Nathan coming to see me today?'

I acted dumb and asked her why she thought that or where she'd heard it. She said she just knew. There were only three of us that knew about the planned surprise so, to this day, I don't know how she found out, but she said she could sense it. At this stage *Beautiful Life* was her album of choice and, as 'Caledonia' played, more tears flowed. Arranging her funeral as we listened to 'Call You Home', I asked her if I could suggest one thing for the final curtain. On 9 September 2017, after ten short weeks and while listening to Nathan's albums, Annie passed away, listening to *Livin' the Dream* and 'Jealous of the Angels'. This was the final song we had chosen from me to her, and it was again very poignant that Nathan would be at our final journey together, as he was on every other one we had ever taken.

So, as the song title says, I am somewhat jealous, as they have taken my best friend, but I also get comfort that they now have another angel.

RIP Annamarie Colton (Glaslough, County Monaghan), 9 September 2017.

– David McCague

Testimonials

Father Brian D'Arcy

Nathan Carter is quite simply a world-class entertainer. I've been lucky enough to be around the entertainment industry for over fifty years. I've seen the best, including Frank Sinatra, live. The only star I wanted to see perform and didn't was the King, Elvis Presley.

Over the years I came to appreciate and admire most of them.

I can assure you that Nathan Carter is now up there with the very best of them.

Firstly, he's a superb singer who can handle the great songs of the modern era. Just when you wonder if he might make the top notes of the classic songs, he effortlessly takes flight and leaves the audience stunned.

He's totally at home on keyboards and, for a relatively slight young man, he has that magic ingredient – *presence*.

I went to see Nathan at his earliest gigs here in Ireland as he started out on his professional career. It was in the cruel recession years when live music was on its knees. It would take a rare talent to survive. The fact that he was born in Liverpool and was risking his future over here made his success even more unlikely.

Did Ireland really need another accordion-playing country singer starting out in the middle of the worst recession in decades?

From the beginning, Nathan had that elusive factor which

connected him with his audience. Of course, there were tough days initially. He was an unknown artist and was young enough to be the grandchild of his earliest fans. Actually, his biggest fans were his grandparents.

Within a year, though, we all recognized that Nathan was an entirely new phenomenon.

Miraculously, he not only appealed to the older generation but won over sceptical teenagers. He enticed a whole new generation to come back to live music and real dancing. He quite simply created a market which no one knew existed.

It was the only time in fifty years that I witnessed the birth of a massive new entertainment niche. It took a combination of exceptional talent, an amazing personality, hard work, determination and good management.

Nathan has brought a level of professionalism rarely seen here. His band is exceptional. He respects his ever-growing audience and he treats them to a night of all-round entertainment. He packs out arenas here and in Britain. The London Palladium on St Patrick's Night followed by the 3Arena in Dublin and then the SSE in Belfast is as big as it gets.

He's a serious talent, and for his dedication, he deserves all the success he's got so far.

I'm proud to call him a friend, and he has helped out many charities and churches of all religions. Music unites us, especially in Northern Ireland. He has, in his own quiet way, brought us all together. He shares his gifts for the good of all.

This wonderful book is just one more inevitable step on the road to international success. He has worked hard and taken many risks to get here. No artist deserves the acclaim more than Nathan Carter, the Irish star from Liverpool, the entertainer supreme, the star who has it all.

Lisa McHugh (country singer)

The first time I remember chatting to Nathan properly was at an awards ceremony at the Tullyglass Hotel in Ballymena many years ago. It was my first time attending a country-music awards event and I knew virtually no one, so when I got talking to Nathan and realized that it was his first awards ceremony too and he knew no one, it was a relief to find someone in the same boat. Nathan had just moved across from Liverpool and I had too, from Scotland, but it was very early days for both of us in our careers and it was great to get chatting to someone who was also trying to find their way on the Irish country scene, not knowing if we would really be accepted, when we were from the UK.

We just hit it off instantly, we really clicked, and we had lots and lots in common, as we had the same dreams, goals and aspirations. We became friends on Facebook and kept in touch, our paths crossing many times after that at different functions and shows, and soon we became very close friends and have stayed that way ever since.

It's great to have someone in the same business to share ideas with, as sometimes you can be so close to a project that you can't see the wood for the trees and it takes an outsider looking in to help you make decisions. I do that for him and he does it for me.

We trust each other, as we do everyone in our circle of friends, and this is very important for someone in the public eye, as you have to be careful sometimes. We all know our boundaries and how to protect each other when we're out and about.

Nathan is so talented, and his success has come from a lot of hard work. I've never met someone so driven. He just has it, whatever it is about him – maybe it's charisma, but it's the full package that has any audience eating out of the palm of his hand, and that doesn't come naturally to many, the way it does to him. It's the same whether he's on a massive stage or just in the corner of a pub enjoying a pint of Guinness and singing in session for a handful of people – everyone just takes to him immediately.

Nathan has a very bubbly personality and I've heard some people who don't know him personally who say the opposite, but the truth is that he can be very shy when he doesn't know someone and it takes him a while to let his guard down but, once you do get to know him, you'll see that he's just a normal guy, and he's always the best person to have at a party or a night out with, as he's full of music and craic.

I've so many great memories from throughout our lengthy friendship and one that stands out is from about four years ago when we were planning, as we do on a regular basis, a group holiday for January. We normally go somewhere like Tenerife, but I fancied venturing a bit further so we put the word out to our friends about a trip to New York and Las Vegas to see who wanted to go. Eventually, the responses all came in and it turned out it was just the two of us, so I told Nathan I didn't mind if he didn't. Of course, we knew it would get tongues wagging as to the idea that we might be a couple again, but we both knew different and really fancied the holiday, so off we went and we had an absolute ball. We enjoyed New York, but Vegas was something else, and we walked around like two kids in a sweet shop, our mouths dropping in awe as we took it all in. One afternoon we were having a drink outside a bar on the strip when I noticed in the near distance some scantily clad, very ripped, muscly men who were having photos taken with tourists, lifting women up between them, and I fancied having a go, so

Nathan was photographer and we laughed our heads off as they picked me up by the armpits, one on either side of me – it was so funny! I dared Nathan to have a picture taken next and, always up for a laugh, he did, and it was a hilarious sight to see his legs dangling between these two giant men. We were both tipsy, which made it even funnier, and it's one of the best photos I've ever seen. Nathan was well on his road to major success at that time, but this showed me that he hadn't changed a bit. To me, he's always just Nathan and, because I've watched his career grow from the very beginning, it's so nice to see that he's still the same inside.

I feel very lucky to have Nathan as one of my best friends and I know that I speak for all of our friends when I say that. He is so good to all of us, he has the biggest heart and he only ever wants everyone to have fun and make the best memories where possible. I'm genuinely so proud of all he has done and achieved since the day we met in the Tullyglass in Ballymena and I have no doubt in my mind that we're only scratching the surface of his success. I'll always have his back and I know that he'll have mine too. I'd be the first to stick up for him if I ever heard anything negative said about him, I'll always support him and I'm very proud to have someone like Nathan Carter in my life.

Jonathan Owens, Spout Studio (music producer/musician)

I first met Nathan when he was playing on the same line-up as Jimmy Buckley, who I was producing at the time, way back when he was very young, maybe about seventeen or eighteen, and he came up to me and said, 'Hello, I'm Nathan. Here's my CD, I'd love to record with you one day.'

I didn't hear back from him until a few years later, when

John Farry had taken him under his wing, and the plan fell into place. The first thing that struck me about him when he first came into my studio was his vast musicality. He is a fantastic musician and so humble with it. He always listens, he is very patient and is interested in the ideas I have as well as his own. I don't think he buys into the whole superstar thing, even though superstardom has certainly found him. He's still the guy that just loves playing music. For me, working with Nathan is a real pleasure, as he is just so easy, due to his knowledge of music, be it on piano, accordion or guitar or in his production ear. He has achieved so much in a relatively short space of time and it's a real honour for me to be a part of his journey.

Nathan is very equal when in the studio. He is trusting and we have a mutual understanding when it comes to laying down tracks. The process is always just me and him, and it really works. I know what he wants by now when he comes to me with a song – we talk about the song, we talk about the type of music we've been listening to and what he finds exciting at the time, and we just seem to hit it off. I think that's the secret to a good relationship between an artist and a producer. If someone comes in and sits with their coat up round their face and doesn't give any feedback, then it makes our job a lot more difficult!

I went along to the 3Arena gig this year in Dublin, and I sat there the whole time with goosebumps and a lump in my throat as I listened to the songs, one after one, and I have to admit I felt proud of them all, and especially of Nathan – it's surreal to see him up there playing in front of almost ten thousand people. No one deserves it more. I texted him after the show to congratulate him and, though he told me off for not telling him I'd be there, I think we shared a moment of great pride. Nathan Carter has made country music cool. I will continue to watch on as he keeps on soaring higher and higher.

Shane Filan (singer, formerly in Westlife)

Working with Nathan Carter and duetting together on 'You Raise Me Up' on his RTÉ show was such a fantastic experience. I've admired his career for a long time and was delighted when my manager, Louis Walsh, asked me to sing with him. We decided to sing 'You Raise Me Up' because it is a very special song to both of us. It was the first time we had met, and we instantly had a rapport, so I knew it would be something special to sing together. I do hope we get to do it again some time.

Tony Allen (Foster and Allen)

Since Nathan came to Ireland a few years ago to be part of the Irish music scene and got the wagon wheels rolling, there has been no stopping him. I'm delighted to see that he is now one of the biggest acts on both the Irish and the international country-music scene, and his success is very well deserved. Both Mick Foster and I were delighted when he agreed to record 'Burning Bridges' with us, and we had a lot of craic, both in the studio recording the song and making the video on location in Belfast.

All the very best, Nathan. You're a real star!

Paul Claffey, Midwest Radio/Ireland West Music TV

The first time Nathan Carter came into our studio, my co-presenter Gerry Glennon and I looked at each other and predicted that he was going to be a big star. Our predictions were right, of course, as Nathan is now one of the brightest stars to shine on the Irish country scene. He has all the qualities one could wish for. He has brought a whole new generation to country music and has expanded the boundaries beyond belief. In our opinion, he is only just starting. Nathan Carter, the world is truly your oyster!

Geraldine Lynch (music teacher)

May 1990 Nathan Carter arrived, both his parents were
    mesmerized.
A beautiful child he grew up to be, but shortly after then
    there were three.
The eldest son to Noreen and Ian, he found his niche at
    school choir singing.
At an early age he started listening to Irish trad and
    country and western.
His grumps (grandad) in the living room, playing
    all sorts –
Big Tom, mainly, and Dolly Parton, of course!
A quick-learning child Nathan came to be, accordion
    bought at the age of three.
Singing and dancing concerts at home, but then grew up
    and started to roam.
To Comhaltas, school choir, over to our house, for the
    craic, a lesson not needed no doubt.
Au natural, Nathan shone through, a lovely young man,
    stardom pursued.
Liverpool home, Ireland close to his heart, 'Wagon
    Wheel', stage lights, he took the part.
An amazing young man with a big heart of gold, never
    forgets friends from days of old.

Well, not that old, I hasten to say, he texts or rings while
    out on his way.
Superstar he is now but never forgets, so genuine, not
    changed him, we are blessed.
So from my heart to yours, a genuine lad, so thoughtful
    and caring, bright lights, helipad
Has not changed the young man from Liverpool, Nathan,
    thank you for all that you do.
We love you and thank you always in mind, for me and
    my family you've always been kind.

Hugo Duncan (BBC Radio Ulster)

I first heard Nathan perform at a concert in Enniskillen and I remember standing there at the side of the stage with Father Brian D'Arcy and marvelling at the talent and vocal ability he had. I could tell he had already come through the ranks of the pub scene, the wedding gigs and small venues, yet he had his feet firmly on the ground. He breathed new life into country music, just like the late Big Tom did in his debut and just like Daniel O'Donnell did when he first started out.

What makes Nathan so special is that he is not just a singer. He is an all-round entertainer who uses every inch of the stage, coming across as a real pro. I recall one event in Castlebar, County Mayo, when I was part of the bill at one of his country weekends. I had performed first with Nathan's band and, when he took to the stage, about two or three songs in, the entire sound and lighting cut out, the security lights came on and there wasn't a thing on stage that hadn't fused. Nathan didn't panic or lose his way. He simply picked up the accordion and sang a few songs, to which the audience joined in. He really had them all in the palm of his hand. To me, that was another sign that this was no ordinary performer, and I even took photos of it all to remember it with.

I play a lot of Nathan's music on my BBC radio show, not only because I enjoy it but also because it's in great demand from the country-music audience, and I remember 'Wagon Wheel' and the major turn of tides that it brought his way. The video had a vibrancy and a sense of youth in it that made us all sit up and listen and watch something fresh and new!

I have so much respect for Nathan Carter and I truly believe he deserves every ounce of success that has come his way to date, and all the success, I have no doubt, that will come his way in the future.

Pio McCann (Highland Radio)

Nathan first called in to us at Highland Radio station and introduced himself and his new CD not long after he had supported Big Tom at the Galtymore, and I was immediately struck by his approach, his great manners and his serious love for country music. Without a doubt, since he came on to the scene, he has lifted our country music here in Ireland out of the doldrums and made it recognizable to people who would never take it under their notice. He made it climb and climb up to where it belongs in Ireland, and now sixteen-year-olds, even four-year-olds, even my own children, who never listened to country music, are Nathan Carter fans. He just has got that modest touch and it's evident the moment he gets up on to the stage that he is so very talented. I was there on his launch night at the Greenvale in Cookstown and I said to him, 'Nathan, never put down that box (accordion) for that's part and parcel of what will bring you right to the top.'

He just oozes energy and generates it to his audience, making the masses who follow him very happy indeed.

He has a great taste in music, and all his years of competing at fleadhs stand by him, plus, his own very varied tastes, which come through in what he plays, and this gives him that universal appeal. He is always so happy when performing – you can see it in his face that he loves every single second of what he does, and he gives every ounce he has into his shows.

Most of all, I'd like to say thank you to Nathan. He came on to our scene and he gave it a big lift, doing every single one of us in the country-music business in Ireland a massive favour. Nathan is a huge star in Ireland, but he will go even further. I believe he will bring his music right across the planet, as he has the complete superstar package that many performers can only dream of.

Big T (Downtown Radio)

I was once asked to introduce a young Nathan Carter on to the stage at an event in the Elk nightclub in Toomebridge, County Antrim. It was a big marquee event and, just before I left, as I was finishing off my radio show, I got a phone call from the venue to announce to the public that there would be no more admission – the place was full up. What made this so remarkable was that it was taking place on one of the wettest nights in my memory and, as I was driving, with the windscreen wipers turned up to the max, I wondered what this singer had that had taken so many people out on such a bad evening. When I got there, I saw there were bouncers taking him under their guard and, when I announced him on to the stage, I don't think anyone in the audience heard a word I said, such was the volume of the screaming fans. I'd never seen anything like it since Joe Dolan! They were reaching out to touch him, calling his name, and I thought to myself, My goodness, this guy has something! I also noticed that the audience was made up of a very wide age range and that he was appealing to all, a lot of the time by making old songs sound like new. It was real crossover stuff. Never had I ever seen such a mixed crowd all singing along and enjoying a concert together. Back at the radio station, Downtown, I approached our head of music and managing director and I told them about this phenomenon. This was our audience, our listeners, not just dancing but going crazy, and we knew we had to do something about it. They finally went to see Nathan for themselves in Armagh and, before long, we took a risk and put on a show called Country Comes to Town at the Europa Hotel in Belfast – a huge risk, but it worked.

Nathan is very accessible, and he doesn't mind having a chat with anyone he meets. My grandchildren adore him – the eight-year-old has been a fan since the age of four, and the four-year-old now is starting to sing along to his songs. Young Adam has a checked shirt, a cowboy hat and boots, and he loves to get his photo taken with Nathan at any opportunity, which Nathan always remembers and he asks about him every time I see him, even remembering that, on one occasion, Adam had his cowboy boots on the wrong feet!

Nathan puts on a live show as if it's a TV extravaganza, and it's like he was born onstage, as he works the audience with his vocals, his piano and his accordion. His family are as warm as he is, and I remember having to announce at a gig that there was to be no dancing, only to be approached by a lady when I was standing at the back of the hall during

the show who insisted I broke the rules and danced with her.
It was Nathan's nan — and I couldn't say no to her, could I?
So off I set for the jive! What you see is what you get with
Nathan. He never changes and is always such a lovely person. I'm delighted to have watched his success so far and
look forward to seeing what comes next for this country
superstar.

Daniel O'Donnell

I first became aware of Nathan when I was given a copy of
his first album. After listening to it I got his phone number
and called him to tell him how much I enjoyed it.

I knew from our conversation that he had a great passion
for his music and he wanted to make it his life career, so I
said to him that he should come to Ireland, as I felt that there
were more opportunities here. Now I'm not sure if he came
here on my recommendation, but whatever made up his
mind it certainly was the way to go!

Since then, I have watched his rise to the top with great
interest. He is a great singer with a stage presence to match.
He really does deserve all his success. A few years ago I met
himself and Lisa McHugh while on holiday in Tenerife. We
were taking a selfie and I said, 'I hope I don't look like your
father.' We went to the Hole in the Wall bar. After a few minutes a man came up to Nathan and said, 'I have all of your
dad's CDs.' Since then, I'm jokingly referred to as 'Dad'.

I have no doubt that Nathan will in a short period become
a household name all over the world, just as he has in Ireland, and I want to take this opportunity to wish him all the
best. Enjoy the journey, Nathan, we certainly are blessed to
be able to do what we love.

When I invited Nathan up on stage all those years ago in Donegal, I had no idea what I was in for musically. There I was, singing away, when I spotted a young, good-looking lad in the front few rows and, to be honest, he stood out like a sore thumb. Let's just say he wasn't the usual clientele to come to my concerts, and it was around the time a big news scandal had broken about an older woman and a younger man and I couldn't resist making a joke about it. The audience called out to me that he was in fact a singer from Liverpool and when he took to the stage and sang 'Don't Close Your Eyes', he totally stole the show and I was gobsmacked.

Nathan has brought the country-music scene to a much younger audience, and seeing the people now jiving to his music reminds me of when I was starting out and when it was a new phenomenon, following the more traditional céilí music scene that most of my generation grew up with. The buzz is back in country, it's cool again and it's so refreshing to see that.

While we entertained in mainly 'dry halls' and carnivals, country singers now sing in big hotel function rooms and very upmarket outdoor festivals that are a far cry off the four- or five-pole tents that we used to think were fancy, with a bit of a curtain (if you were lucky!) to change behind.

From the moment I first met Nathan, I've always found him to be a very level-headed lad who loves the craic. Nathan wasn't a novice when he first came to Ireland. He had earned his trade from the pubs, Irish centres and functions in England and all his time with Nicky James, which has really stood by him. I listened to him just recently when we did a show in the Shetlands together – instead of rushing around,

I just stopped and had a really good listen, and his voice is so wonderful. He just goes for it onstage and makes it seem so natural, which to him it, essentially, is.

A lot of people expect overnight success when they come into this business, but Nathan has worked his way to the very top and he deserves every bit of it. He gives his audience exactly what they want, and that's the most important craft of all.

Ryan Tubridy (Presenter of RTÉ's The Late Late Show*)*

When Nathan first sang as a guest on *The Late Late Show*, I could sense there was quite a buzz around this young musician from Liverpool. He was on to something big and it was clear he wasn't just here for the weekend!

We've always had a rich tapestry of 'country and Irish' singers here in Ireland who have represented the genre for many years with brilliance, but it was evident that it needed a reboot, an injection of new blood, and Nathan led the way with this, re-energizing the scene with other younger singers like Mike Denver and, more recently, the likes of Cliona and Derek Ryan, among others. He has brought country music to a new generation – and to people like me.

As I drove around towns and cities I'd see posters for singers like Nathan who were packing in audiences and filling halls all over the place and I thought that it was time *The Late Late Show* acknowledged and embraced this, so with our head of music, Dermot McEvoy, we knocked on doors, asked to be friends and we were met with great warmth and enthusiasm. From that, *The Late Late Show Country Special* was born.

From Big Tom, to Daniel and to Nathan and many more, we try to represent all generations and we aim to give these singers the respect and admiration they deserve.

Nathan Carter connects to his audience. He is authentic. He has great energy and he always picks the right songs to sing. He has a spark about him and a youthful demeanour that has a wide appeal to all who hear him. Sometimes in this business, the good guy succeeds.

I really do believe that Nathan Carter is one of the good guys.

Nicky James

When Nathan sings, it is instantly brilliant. I never had any doubt after first hearing him that he was going to be a big star. I worked with him on his very first recording as a producer and performer and I always believed that he had it, whatever 'it' is. Some call it the X factor, but whatever it is, he has it. Nathan also has the ability to make everyone who meets him feel like they've known him all their lives. He has always been approachable and there's no falseness with Nathan. People like him everywhere he goes, and he gives so much back to the people who support him. Around the time when I first met him, my eldest son tragically died, and working with Nathan really helped me get through those darkest of years. He's very busy now, but we still keep in touch a lot. For me, it was written in the stars for Nathan. He ticks all the boxes – not just with his talent, but with the whole package of things, even down to his strong family background and the support they give him. I was with him the day he signed with his Irish management, and I think I was more excited than he was! All the links in the chain came together for him, everyone he met brought him on a step further and, when we left Ireland that day after his first meeting, I remember thinking, This is going to be great. As they say, the rest is history.

John Farry

Monday, 4 May 2009: Gateway Hotel, Buncrana, County Donegal.

Charity concert with special guests Louise Morrissey, Gene Stuart, Nathan Carter, Seamus McGee, John Farry and the Ryan Turner Band ...

I remember hearing the advert for the concert on Highland Radio. I was really delighted to be asked to perform on this show, and it was all down to the fact that Highland Radio had been giving really good airplay to 'Mother's Birthday Song' (a song that I had written for my mum, Kathleen), which subsequently led to local promoter Tommy Cunningham and radio presenter Stephen Lynch giving me a call to perform on the show.

When I look back now, I realize that my mum's song was the real reason I was there, and I often wonder about the part that fate played in all of this. Thanks, Mum xx!!

I was really looking forward to this gig as it meant getting to sing some of my own songs with a good backing band, instead of my usual solo singer-songwriter gig in smaller venues throughout the north-west of Ireland.

I remember I was one of the first artists on stage, as I guess I was one of the lesser-known acts, but as I didn't get to perform at these events very often I thought I would wait around and hear all of the other acts also, and maybe sell a few CDs after the show.

And then a young singer from Liverpool, Nathan Carter, was introduced on stage ... I remember watching his performance and I could not believe the quality of the voice. How could such a young man with such a slight build have such a rich vocal that belied his teenage years?

Nathan performed five songs that night, and he simply had the crowd in the palm of his hand from the first song to his last.

One song in particular I remember was the Joe Dolan classic, 'The Answer to Everything', and how prophetic was that!

Immediately after the show I got to meet young Nathan for the first time, and we got talking about new songs, a new band, and new career plans, much of which has already been documented in this book, and I suppose it's fair to say that a little bit of Irish country-music history was made that night.

I can honestly say that, from that very first meeting, we have got along exceptionally well together, and while we don't agree on everything, I believe that we work really well as a team, and long may that continue.

I don't believe that I have ever met anyone who is as driven, determined and totally focused on what he wants to do in his musical career, and to be all of those things and yet remain a very level-headed, loyal, sincere and genuine guy is a pretty rare thing. He's also someone I regard as a good friend – but it's still all true!

I do keep telling him, though, that once he has achieved something big he should stop occasionally and smell the roses, but Nathan is always too busy climbing to the top of the next hill and looking to see where the next big mountain he can climb is.

Nathan's career continues to evolve, as it has from his dance-hall days, and who knows where his career will take him? But I guess that's for the next book!

All I do know is that, whatever he does, he will give it 110 per cent every night and every time.

I'm proud to say that I discovered Nathan Carter, and I

like to think that I have been of some help to him on his musical journey, but I will leave that for others to judge.

This book is a fitting tribute to a true star and, when it came to picking the title for the book, I guess I could think of only one title that really said it all, because Nathan Carter was born to sing. He was born for the road.